Retriever Training *for Spaniels*

Working with soft-tempered, hard-headed, intelligent dogs

Pamela Owen Kadlec

JUST DUCKY

PUBLISHING

Retriever Training for Spaniels
by Pamela Owen Kadlec

Just Ducky Publishing
P.O. Box 129
Edgefield, South Carolina 29824

Publishers Cataloging-in-Publication
(Provided by Quality Books, Inc.)
Kadlec, Pamela Owen.
    Retriever training for spaniels : working with soft-tempered, hard-headed, intelligent dogs/Pamela Owen Kadlec, - - 1st ed.
    p.cm
    Includes index.
    ISBN 0-9717103-0-9
    1. Spaniels –Training 2. Hunting dogs– Training
    1. Title
    SF429.S7K33 2002   636.752'435
                                 QB102-200232

Cover design by Brent Cline
Edited by David F. Johnson
Indexing by Michelle Graye - Indexing and Reference Services
Printed by Publishers' Graphics
Front cover photos by author: Springer spaniel - Gabby Ann Mealing, AWS - SHR UH Waterway's Dax WD, Boykin spaniel - HRCH UH Curlee Gurlee
Back cover: Biography photo by Millie Latimer
Back cover photo of four Boykins by Brenda Thornton
Photos in the book are by the author unless otherwise indicated
Hunt Test title statistics compiled in January, 2002

Dedication

This book is dedicated to all of my dog loving friends, some who have trained with me, others who inspired me to write this book, including:

◆My son, Kristopher. Follow your dreams.

◆R.K. "Strick" and Roger Strickland, without whom this book would not be possible.

◆Millie and Jim Latimer, of Rock'n Creek Kennel, two great friends who gave me my start in South Carolina so I could be closer to all the Little Brown Dogs.

◆Mark Fulmer, of Sarahsetter Kennel, a good friend and trainer who also believes in the clicker.

◆Betsy Reiney and Karen Spencer, my Florida training partners who own those big retrievers but appreciate all the little dogs can do.

◆And of course, HRCH UH Curlee Gurlee, who taught me about spaniels and spaniel temperaments, which has made me a better person and trainer.

HRCH UH Curlee Gurlee

Just Ducky's Justmyluck - "Lucky"
Sire: 2000 BSS National Intermediate Champion
Twisted Creek's Drake
Dam: HRCH UH Curlee Gurlee

Contents

Foreword

Over the years I have been lucky in having many good, easily trained dogs. Usually from well-bred retriever and spaniel lines, they have a temperament that matches my own that makes them easy to work with and train. Even with the occasional difficult one I have found that a patient trainer will eventually be able to work the dog to a standard that would allow me to take them out with confidence in the shooting field.

Where I have had difficulties is with the dogs that seem to be a mixture of temperaments. They are soft in that you cannot put too much pressure on them, and they are hard headed in that they can on occasions be stubborn. They are capable of deciding what to do on their own in the field, which can be a problem if what they want to do is not what you want them to do. This type of dog can become an excellent hunting companion but is usually difficult to train by standard methods. Such dogs, however, often have the ability to find that difficult bird using their own initiative and determination when you leave them to their own devices. I have found that much of their personality comes from being thinking dogs. In this book Pam terms them *intelligent* and there is no doubt that they reason and make decisions on their own. Given the right training these dogs can become good working gun dogs.

Some trainers enjoy the rewards of working with these dogs. Pam is one and one of the best. To do this she uses several approaches and methods to bring out the best in such a dog. Her approach is creative and anticipates what the dog will be thinking and doing in response to any training or field situation. In training intelligent dogs, Pam does not stick to a single, inflexible approach. In this book she uses her considerable experience to explain many different methods and approaches. You have to get the dog to want to be your partner and to need you in his life to get the retrieving pleasures he seeks.

This is a book for both novice owner and those who have trained spaniels before and now wish to improve their abilities to train their dogs for retrieving. It is an extremely practical guide to dog training. Pam has an ability not only to train but also explain clearly how to do so. Watching her at hunt tests working her Boykin spaniels I realize how much she is at one with them. She understands their temperaments and does not make excuses for their characters. She is never fooled by them and knows exactly how they think.

Easy to read and understand, this book is will help anyone wishing to train his or her spaniel to retrieve. If your dog has a mind of its own, this is the book for you.

Martin Deeley
International Gundog Workshops
Author, Writer, Commentator, International Gundog Trainer
Montverde, Florida and Poole, England

Irish Water Spaniel
U-CDX Saracen's Bold to the Bone CDX JH WCX CGC
photo by Holly Thau

American Water Spaniel
SHR UH Waterway's Dax. WD

Chapter 1
Overview

This book is for the Boykin and other spaniel owners who are looking for specific information on training their dog in non-slip retriever work. A non-slip retriever is one that stays in place when the bird is shot and doesn't fetch until commanded to do so - he doesn't *slip his lead*.

There are many great books on training your spaniel to flush and tons of them on training retrievers, but none that addresses the temperament of the spaniel. Training a spaniel is different from training a Labrador retriever. Most Labs are what I call 'push-button' dogs. You push a button and they go, usually in the direction you sent them. The temperament of a Lab is great: they can take almost any kind of treatment and still turn out to be nice hunting dogs. Some of them even respond better to a heavy-handed approach. The field trial Labs have been bred to withstand hot electronic collar corrections, however, and are too high powered for the average hunter/handler.

Spaniels are very intelligent, and are typically soft-tempered dogs. If you work with your pup as in a progressive school – that is, letting pup advance at his own rate – you will have fun training him. If you try to push your pup too fast past his abilities, you will end up butting heads. Some spaniels will be steady and delivering birds to hand by six months. Some will be doing doubles and simple blind retrieves by seven months. Most will take a little more time to mature and gain confidence. The soft, timid pups require patience on the part of their owner. They don't need to be babied. Just the opposite. They need to have plenty of birds and excitement to get them fired up for hunting.

The spaniel is a flushing dog. He quarters. He does not take a straight line to the bird. Pup will start off straight, maybe for 30 yards, then the nose will drop (or raise, depending on the dog) and he'll work in a zigzag pattern hunting the bird. The flushing instinct that drives spaniels to quarter back and forth has a purpose: a quartering dog covers a lot of ground while still hunting close to his master. The dog's instinct to quarter, however, makes it difficult to teach a spaniel to take a line for a mark and especially for a blind retrieve. It makes it difficult to get the dog to sit on a whistle and take directions. Your spaniel knows (at least he thinks he does) much better than you do where the bird is! I can hear him now, "The bird is obviously in that clump of bushes over there! Don't bother me with all that whistling, can't you see I'm busy?"

The typical spaniel is both soft-tempered and hard-headed. You will get into many power struggles along the way. Soft-tempered means that if you put too much pressure on the dog or if you use excessive negative reinforcement – hitting or hot e-collar stimulation – the dog will shut down on you. You will be left with a couch potato at best, a fear biter at worst. If you lose your temper easily then do not get a spaniel. Dogs do not respond well to anger and this relates particularly to spaniels. They don't bounce back, and some even hold grudges. Honest.

Boykins and most other spaniels respond much better to positive reinforcement. But sometimes a good yank on the check cord is needed or the pup will take advantage of your good nature. Spaniels are very smart dogs and they will test you to see if you are paying attention. ***The trick is finding the right balance.***

This book will aid you in finding that balance and training your dog to be a wonderful hunting companion and well-behaved house dog.

Chapter 2

Basic Tenets of Dog Training

All dog trainers have their own methods of training that work for them. These methods may not be unique; in fact, they are most likely a combination of several methods. You will learn to read your dog and use the advice that works best for your dog. Each animal is an individual, just like people, and will move through different stages of development at different rates. If your dog doesn't respond to one training method, try another. Don't give up on your dog just because he doesn't conform to a set standard. Learn to adapt and grow with your pup and you will both have a wonderful life together.

The following tenets are basic rules that work no matter what methods you use.

Keep a Journal

Each day write down what pup did during each training session. In your notes, include the time, the weather conditions, whether the training was on land or water, whether you used birds or bumpers, which training partners were present, what kind of work you did (puppy retrieves, marks, blinds, etc.) and details about how pup performed. For example, did he drop his birds, run off with the bird, or come straight back to you? Keeping precise notes will be invaluable, particularly later when you move to advanced work. You can start off with a simple spiral notebook or you can design a more formal training log entry, like the sample included in this chapter. Journal page sample courtesy of Chris Meurett, owner of HR Just Ducky's Tourbillion and Just Ducky's Justforkicks. Chris has filled several books with the work he does with his 'boys'.

Focus on the Job at Hand

Always keep your eyes on your dog. Don't look away or be distracted by talking to your buddies while pup is working. The second you look away you break the invisible line that is pulling pup in to you. It's true, especially of spaniels. If you look away, the next thing you know pup is dropping his birds, taking a shortcut by land rather than water, or even taking off to enjoy his bird for lunch.

Food for Thought

Positive reinforcement using food treats works. Don't knock it until you try it. I used to think food treats were for sissies and fools. Not any more. I would also suggest that you get the book, *Don't Shoot the Dog* by Karen Pryor, and learn about clicker training. I use the clicker and treats on all my puppies and gradually fade it out once the behavior is conditioned. If you use a clicker and positive reinforcement to condition the pup, the pup will sit on every whistle without thinking about it - he simply can't help himself. It is a joy to work with your pup when you can see the wheels turning in his head, as he tries to think about what he can do to make *you* click.

The clicker also works wonders on incredibly soft dogs. You know the one: the dog that slinks on his belly to greet you, pees on the floor, or rolls on his back. Sometimes this behavior is the dog's response to abuse, but often it's just the dog's nature. The owners have inadvertently reinforced this behavior by pampering the dog rather than ask for bolder behavior. In the clicker training chapter (Chapter 7) we will discuss how to modify the behavior of the soft dog.

Fifteen-Minute Lessons

You can train your dog to do finished gun dog work by spending only fifteen minutes a day working with him. The key to all dog training is consistency. If you always expect compliance to your commands, and enforce those commands promptly, your dog will learn to listen.

Every time you take your dog outside (or let him out of his kennel), have him sit. Every time you open a door or gate, have him sit. Every time you walk out of the door or gate, have pup stay seated until you release him. At first it may take the entire fifteen minutes just to teach the sit. Then, it may take another day (or week) and another fifteen minutes each lesson just to teach him to sit and wait for you to release him. But, once he learns those lessons you will spend one or two minutes reminding pup to sit and wait and the other thirteen minutes teaching pup to fetch or heel, or come when called.

Take advantage of feeding times. Use this time to work pup on basic obedience. It is so easy to use pup's mealtime as a reinforcement tool, feeding him a handful at a time when he sits, stays, comes, kennels, or lies down on command.

If you take those few extra minutes every time you feed, pup can also learn patience and start learning the concept of *steady*. When the food is almost gone from your mini lessons, start teaching pup *steady*. Have him sit before you put his food down and eventually he'll stay seated until you release him by speaking his name. At first you will need to grab his collar with one hand and restrain him while you place his food dish down with your other hand. As with all lessons, give pup time to understand what you expect from him.

Imagine how much more you could teach pup with *two* fifteen- minute lessons a day. Of course, this all works best if you have the land and water for training in your backyard. Otherwise, you can still concentrate on all the basics and yard work during the week and stretch pup out on weekends or evenings when you have time to drive to your training grounds.

Temper, Temper

Never train your dog if you are in a bad mood. Stop training your dog if you lose your temper. The damage may be irreparable.

If you lose your temper, stop and take a deep breath. Give the pup an easy command so that you can end the lesson on a good note. Put the pup up and quit for the day.

There will be times that you have to work through a problem. You know your dog and will be able to read him to tell when to stop and when to push on. Follow your instincts. Most times you will simply back up and make the lesson easier before advancing to the next lesson.

If you lose your temper with your dog or use too much pressure the pup may refuse to work. This is called *shutting down.* The dog just quits and won't play any more. When this happens and you can't work through the problem the best solution is to put the dog in the kennel and let him chill out. This may take a week, a month or six months. If it's a no-go situation where the dog refuses to retrieve, don't ask him to (unless the dog is in the middle of the conditioned retrieve, in which case you need to work through the problem).

The day may come when the dog refuses to listen during a hunt. Take into consideration the weather - extreme heat or cold - and the condition of your pup. If he refuses you he may just be worn out from working hard fetching all of your birds. Dogs do not have the ability to scheme out ways to aggravate you. Getting mad and beating your pup for not behaving according to your standards will not help the situation - it will make it worse, and you may even cause irreparable damage. If the dog won't work, put him back in the truck and call it a day. Think about why pup behaved like he did and solve the problem by training.

If you have decided to give pup some time out, but feel the need to do *something*, then concentrate on basic obedience or try your hand at agility. Or, just let the dog relax and do nothing for awhile. Some dogs need time out to mature. Some need confidence. Still others need you to back off on the pressure and just have some fun for awhile. If this is the case, make sure you don't give him any retrieves that result in his establishing bad habits. For example, he is dropping his birds, don't give him any birds until he can reliably deliver a dummy to hand in a controlled setting.

Do Not Follow a Time Line

Any books or advice that tell you that your dog should be doing certain tasks by a certain age will only frustrate you. Do not compare your pup to your buddy's pup. Just like children, each dog is different, has its own personality, its own little quirks. The typical spaniel matures at about 3 years of age and comes into his prime at about 4 or 5. You will have many years of pleasurable hunting with your dog, so don't rush it.

Show and Tell

Always give the dog the benefit of the doubt. If you are not sure whether pup understands a lesson, he probably doesn't. Realize that dogs do not transfer knowledge easily. What this means is just because pup does perfect retrieves in your back yard does not mean he will do them perfectly in the dove field or even in your own front yard. Once you teach pup to sit and heel in the backyard, move to the front yard. Then, move to the area Dog Park. Take him to a kid's soccer or baseball game with all the distractions. Then, move to a field. Then, move to another field. The same with water work. Don't use the same pond every session for training and then expect pup to perform well in a strange pond at a hunt test or duck hunt.

Learn to keep your mouth shut and show the dog what you expect. I'll get into this further on the marked retrieves and blind retrieve chapters.

Do Not Repeat Yourself

If the dog does not come when you say, "Here," you go to the dog, pick up the check cord and pull the dog towards you. When the dog is in front of you, praise her and say, "Good here." Think about it. If you continually repeat yourself the dog will be conditioned to respond to the third or fourth command. As you repeat the command, your voice gets louder and deeper until you are probably shouting, "*HERE*!" By that time, pup thinks, "Well, I guess I should come in now" and responds. Instead, if you say, "Here" in a normal tone of voice that pup can hear, and the dog doesn't respond, you go to the dog and enforce compliance calmly and quietly, the dog gets conditioned to respond on the first command. Treat for compliance. The key is to make it worth the dog's while to come when called. You have to be *more important* and *more exciting* than *anything* else in the world. I know, much easier said than done.

If You Can't Enforce it, Don't Say it

Pup gets wind of a rabbit or deer and is high-tailing it through the woods in hot pursuit. Do not yell, "*Here*," at the top of your lungs and expect compliance. If you get it, pick your jaw up off the ground and praise the heck out of pup. Most likely you will be wasting your breath. If you are not prepared to follow

Journal Page Sample

Date _____ Start Time _____ Finish Time _____

Location _____ Weather Condition _____

Water _____ Land _____ Combination _____

Training Partners _____

Equipment Utilized: Shotgun _____ Blank Pistol _____

Hand Launcher _____ Remote Winger No. ____ Blinds No. _____

Birds _____ Dummies _____ Dokken Ducks _____

Primary Training Activity: Marks _____ Blinds _____

Lining/Casting _____ Anti-Banking _____ Other _____

Explanation _____
_____

Test Set-Up Diagram:

Retriever Performance: _____
_____

Attitude: _____

Notes: _____
_____
_____

through and get the dog to obey, then keep your mouth shut. If pup is running off after prey and you want him to come in you have two options. One is to yell, "Here" once and then go after him (hopefully he has his check cord on or it's in your hand.) The other is to wait him out and let him return on his own. There actually is a third option but we won't be getting into electric collars in this book.

Another example – pup has been on the bench and you have conditioned the retrieve. You moved to the ground and pup took to that as well. It was easy to correct any problems. You move to the water and pup: a) refuses to go into the water, or b) goes in but refuses to pick up the bumper. What do you do? Go swimming, of course.

Never give a command you can't enforce.

Sit, Sit, Sit

Sit before you open the door to go in or out. Sit before the food is put down. Sit at heel. Sit to the whistle. Sit to the flush. Sit to the shot. Sit and stay sitting until you say otherwise. Sit and stay until you say pup's name to release him to eat. Sit and stay until you say pup's name to release him to retrieve. You get the idea. Make sure pup does.

Be consistent. Always have pup sit before any activity, whether it's mealtime or play time.

Make the mealtime an opportunity to work on sit to the whistle. Use pup's kibble as a treat and walk around the yard, whistle in your mouth, tooting and treating until the food is all gone. This teaches pup to sit away from you as well as by your side. If pup moves up toward you when you toot the whistle, move toward pup with your hand upraised (like a traffic cop) and toot again. Praise pup and treat him when he sits. When pup learns the game, only treat once in a while, then gradually fade out the treats all together.

Baby, It's Cold Outside

I know I say to bring your dog into the house and make him a part of the family. The amendment to that is common sense. If you want to take your pup duck hunting in the winter, don't let him stay in a heated house at night and take him to freezing water in the morning. You aren't doing him any favors. Keep pup outside - with a well-insulated doghouse and some straw - so that he gets acclimated to the cold.

The same goes for summer. If pup lies on the air conditioning vent all summer and you take him dove hunting opening day, he will most likely make a beeline for the truck! If he does stick around and work, you may lose your hunting buddy to the heat. Spaniels handle the heat well, but they are dogs, not machines. Too many dogs die from getting overheated in the field. Keep pup conditioned all year round with training so that pup is ready physically and mentally for hunting season. Even with a well-conditioned dog, make sure you have plenty of water to keep your pup hydrated.

Pup can come in the house and socialize, play with the kids and then go outside for the night.

Too Tired to Work?

If pup is distracted or doesn't show any interest in work, ask yourself why. Is pup playing all day with your children or your other dogs? You don't need to keep pup kenneled all day but he does need quiet time (three or four hours before training) so that he is ready to work when you are.

Too Wired to Work?

The opposite of the tired out pup is the wired pup. He's been in his kennel all day and now he's ready to play! Do not let pup run free for fifteen or twenty minutes before you and the pup start working. Ask for and expect control (within reason for puppies) even when the dog is excited. He'll be excited when he hunts and at hunt tests, and you'll need control then, so start conditioning him now. Before letting him out of the kennel, command, 'sit,' and work on this until pup will maintain the sit until you release him by name. Keep pup at heel out of the gate, on lead if necessary, and walk calmly in the yard. Heel pup around for a few minutes and then release him to air (go to the bathroom.) Once pup has aired, get him back in control. Then start the lesson or load him in the truck to go train.

16 - week old Boykin pup, Pat Doc Holiday II - "Doc,"
retrieving a pigeon

Boykin pup with wood duck - photo by An McQuaig

Chapter 3
Picking a Pup
Spaniels vs. Retrievers: Is a Spaniel the Right Dog for Me?

Before picking out the individual pup, first you must decide if a spaniel is the right dog for you. If you mostly hunt small water and flooded timber for your ducks then the spaniel is perfect. If you love to hunt dove and upland game birds, the spaniel is your dog. If you hunt big water and require a dog who can break ice, then get a Chesapeake Bay or Labrador retriever.

If you want the perfect house pet who is great with children, get either a spaniel or a retriever. If you want to keep all the stuff on your coffee table get a spaniel. If you like a clean coffee table, get a Labrador - his constantly wagging tail will dust for you.

If you have an even temperament and can remain calm in times of stress (training smart dogs can try your patience), then get a spaniel. If you can't control your temper, don't get a dog, get a punching bag.

Picking a Pup

There are several theories on picking out the perfect puppy. Pick the one who makes eye contact. Pick the one who doesn't mind being on his or her back. Pick the one who comes to you first. Pick the one that's the most outgoing.

If the breeder is conscientious and raised the litter with daily hands-on play and handling, let the breeder pick out the pup for you. Who knows better the personality of the each pup than the person who has one-on-one experience with the puppies for the past seven weeks? When I raise a litter, each pup is picked up and handled several times each day, including being turned over on its back, held up high, and patted on the rump. Each pup has a collar and short line attached at three weeks so that the litter mates pull and tug on each other. Each pup has been introduced to bird wings and later birds to evaluate his or her desire to hunt. By seven weeks, each pup has retrieved his or her first whole pigeon. Weather permitting, each pup has been swimming. I can tell you which pup is the quietest and which one is the hell-raiser.

If your breeder doesn't do all the above with his puppies, then pick the one your gut tells you is the right one. Take a bird wing with you to tease and play with the pups. Visit the litter one time before you go to take your baby home if at all possible. Take your time. This baby is going to be with you for years, so get the one you connect with.

Battle of the Sexes

Do you get a boy or a girl pup? There are pros and cons for either so it really comes down to personal preference. Some people prefer males since they think they make better hunters. Some prefer females since they have the reputation

HR Just Ducky's Justasample - Sammy

HR UH Sydney of Woodbine x HRCH UH King's Curlee Gurlee

(dam of HR Just Ducky's Tourbillion and SHR Just Ducky's Justdoit)

of being easier to train. With spaniels, I haven't found that much difference between the two. There are hard-charging females and sweet, sissy boys.

If you choose a female, you will have to contend with her heat cycles unless you spay her. On the plus side, you can raise a litter of puppies once you get all the health clearances and the pup is at least two years of age. As a general rule, females are easier to train and less likely to wander away from home.

Males can be hard to housebreak because they feel obligated to mark their territory. Speaking of territory, males have a tendency to wander more than females. The plus side to male dogs is that once he turns two years of age and you get all his health clearances, you can stud him out and not have to worry about puppies.

Size can be a factor for some hunters, and if it is for you, generally males are larger than females. While there may be one or two occasions where bigger is better, 28-pound, 14-inch tall HRCH UH Curlee Gurlee has proven size doesn't matter.

Consider the above factors but keep in mind that each dog is an individual. They won't necessarily fit neatly into a box labeled *boy* or *girl* personalities. They are only tendencies. A lot of the pup's personalities can be attributed to his or her parents and grandparents. That's why it is important to at least meet the parents.

Meet the Parents

If at all possible, see both parents and check out their temperaments. If the dogs are working dogs, ask to see a demonstration of their abilities. The breeder should be happy to show off his or her dogs. Ask for *written* verification of hip and eye clearances. The hips should be OFA or PennHIP certified and the eyes need to be CERF'ed normal. Both OFA (http://www.offa.org) and CERF (http://www.vmdb.org) have databases where you can look up individual dogs to verify certification. Some breeds have other hereditary problems you need to be aware of before buying a puppy.

See if your breed has concerns with temperament, skin disorders, heart problems, elbow or thyroid problems. Do your homework. Ask for referrals from previous puppy buyers. If this is the dam's first litter, check into whether the sire has any pups from other litters and talk to the puppy owners. Look into the background to see if the grandparents were OFA and CERF certified.

Canine Hip Dysplasia (CHD) is a degenerative disease and no breeder can one-hundred percent guarantee sound hips. Even dogs from generations of OFA certified hips can throw a pup with the disease. So, why bother to make sure the parents are OFA or PennHIP certified? Because getting a pup from certified dogs improves your chances of getting healthy dogs.

Are the parents hunting dogs? Many spaniels are great house pets and never see a bird or hear the sound of a shotgun. Bloodlines do tell. Get a pup out of proven hunting bloodlines. Not only birdiness shows here, but train-ability as well. It takes an intelligent dog to be a worthy hunting companion, one with the ability to learn.

Abitt of Hellcat (Cougar)
English springer spaniel pup at 8 weeks
photo by Angela Monaghan

14 month old Sussex spaniel, Emma
CH. Windsong Emerald Dove at Webbfoot, CGC
Photo by Lil Webb

Chapter 4

Housebreaking Pup

You've found the perfect pup and have brought her home. Ideally, you have brought her into *your* home. Forget all those old stories about not letting your hunting dog be a house dog. Boykin spaniels (any breed for that matter) are at their best when they are part of the family.

She's about eight weeks old. The first weeks are a period of adjustment for all of the family members, but the pup will be making the greatest number of adjustments. Lots of love, consistency, and patience are called for. Give the pup time to explore her new world but also start teaching her right from wrong. If she starts chewing on something she's not supposed to (like your favorite hunting boots), tell her 'no' firmly and give her something else to chew on. If she piddles on the floor, *and you catch her in the act*, firmly say "No, *outside*," and take her out.

If you don't catch her in the act she won't know what she is being punished for. If you want to her relieve herself in the same area take her there and tell her 'stool' or 'potty' or 'hurry up' or whatever command you prefer. Realize that a young pup doesn't have much bladder control, so don't fly off the handle and smack the pup hard for something she doesn't understand or can't control yet. Walk her often and every time she wakes up. Walk her immediately after she eats. Pick up all food and water by 6:00 p.m. and walk her before you go to bed. Don't expect her to hold her bladder for 7-8 hours. She can't and it's not healthy for her.

Have her crate placed in an area that is readily accessible to her and leave the door open when she is allowed free time. Put her in the crate with the command, "Kennel." Leave her in the crate for a little while at a time when you are home. Give her a bone or chew toy to keep her occupied. Expect her to cry at first, but if it gets excessive, tell her "Quiet" or "No noise." (Almost) never let pup out of the crate when she's crying. That will only teach her that crying means she can get out! The exception is when she has been crated for a long time and needs to relieve herself. If she cries at night, take her out, praise her for a job well done, and put her back in the crate without a lot of fuss.

At night it sometimes helps to put an old wind-up ticking clock next to the crate with her. The ticking simulates a heartbeat. Another trick is to put one of your worn (you know, the old, torn, sweaty one you had on yesterday) shirts in with her. It has your scent and can soothe her. Most dogs won't soil their sleeping place but again, realize that puppies don't have their bladder and bowels under control. If she continually cries, take her outside and see if she has to relieve herself. When she goes, heap lots of praise on her and put her right back into the crate. Don't play with her; just say "Kennel" (and I use "Bedtime" so they learn that it's time to sleep). Eventually she will come to accept the crate as her home and safe place and will even go into it during the day to rest.

Keep the pup in the crate or a contained area when you are not home. When you are home and are too busy to watch pup, don't leave her loose in the house to get into trouble. Take the time to work with pup and give her exercise before crating her back up. She's been waiting all day for you to come home and play with her.

Springer spaniel
Gabby Ann Mealing

Boykin spaniel pups

Top: Rock' n Creek Duncan

Bottom: Rock' n Creek Knocks

Chapter 5

Puppy Kindergarten

Tools of the trade

- ✓ Collar, six-foot lead, two-foot check cord, and a twenty-five foot check cord
- ✓ Canvas puppy bumpers
- ✓ Birds
- ✓ Journal

By the time the pup is about five or six months old you will start to expect a little obedience from pup. I don't expect you to be a drill sergeant (he is a puppy after all) but you can start to teach him right from wrong. When you let pup out, start to use control. Don't expect one-minute sits and three-minute downs, but get pup used to waiting a second or two before moving. Make him sit before you open the kennel gate or crate door. At first you will need to go into the kennel and restrain pup by holding his collar and getting him to sit. Snap the check cord on. Say his name to release him the same time you let go of the collar. With the check cord in hand, have him walk *easy* out into the yard. If you turn pup out and let him run rampant for the first few minutes of your training session, then he will be harder to settle down and get serious when it really counts.

The key to dog training is to always set the dog up for success. If he doesn't fail, then he doesn't learn any bad habits. Almost all behaviors are learned. The owners teach bad habits, usually inadvertently. Retriever training is a thinking game. Before you do anything with your pup, think about the consequences. If you chase pup to get the bird, he'll learn to play keep-away. If you grab at the bird when pup comes in, he will learn to dance away or drop the bird. If you turn pup out and let him have his head for the first 5-10 minutes of each training session, you are conditioning him to being able to play first, work later. A *work-first* attitude is not as important now as it will be later but it's not too early to start good habits.

By the time your pup is 5 months old he could be sitting to a whistle, coming when called, kenneling on command, walking on lead, swimming like a champ, and retrieving birds. He may already be introduced to gunfire. He will have learned that he gets to go fetch on his name. Using his name to release him to fetch has benefits. One is that because pup only goes when he hears his name, so teaching him to be steady is easier. When pup is in the field (or at a hunt test) with other dogs and another handler says, "Back" (a common command for sending dogs on a retrieve) your pup doesn't take off. Later, when you teach blind retrieves, the back command means to turn around and go back to pick up a bird. You can say anything you like - fetch it, get it, or peanut butter - but it's best to keep it simple and use pup's name.

None of pup's work will be perfect, but he will have a great foundation for future training. As a professional trainer, I see all shapes and sizes of dogs, smart ones and even the occasional drop-out who can't seem to find their own food dish. A truly untrainable dog is a rarity, especially among Boykins, because the average Boykin spaniel is a very intelligent dog. The cause of unresponsiveness in a spaniel is likely to be that the young dog has had no formal training at home. He doesn't sit, he jumps up on everyone, he doesn't heel, and he doesn't listen. Basically, he has no manners! For some reason people have the idea that if you start training a pup too soon, he will lose out on puppyhood. Wrong. Just think of children who learn foreign languages so easily. The same holds true with pups and basic commands. When presented with the chance, a pup will learn very fast and you can make it fun.

Use a flat buckle-type collar on pup. Don't use one of those quick release collars since they break easily. Make sure your check cords are free of knots (other than the one holding the snap) so that pup doesn't get snagged on brush when he's running around.

You will only need one or two small canvas puppy bumpers and two or three knobby bumpers to start. The Dokken dead fowl, teal size, are ideal bumpers for young spaniels. When you advance to blind retrieves you will want a dozen each of white and orange bumpers. I like to have a few of the extra large bumpers, and even one or two of the Dokken Mallards to get pup used to carrying heavier game.

Start your journal

Each day write down what you and pup do. It will be simple stuff now and you can just write down notes in a notebook. Later you will want to draw actual diagrams of the marks and/or blinds, delineating the line the dog took to and from the bird. You can look back and see the progress or where the problem first developed, and perhaps the cause of the problem. Get in the habit now! See the sample journal page in Chapter 2.

Walks

Take your pup for long walks in the woods, playing follow the leader. You are the leader for now. Do not bypass fallen trees, gullies, and streams. Go over under and through anything in your path. Go out of your way to find brush to crawl through, some fallen trees to go under, others to jump over. When you get to an obstacle and you step over it and the pup stops and whines or yips at you do *not* pick her up. Talk to her, encourage her, and let her to figure it out. Start walking away. If she still can't do it, go back and show her again by you stepping over the obstacle. If you show her how to go around it, you may regret it later when she tries to find the easy way out.

Once the pup gets a little braver at this game, she will start going out ahead of you. That is great. When she gets too far out, remind her to come back in. I use 'here, here' or 'hunt close'. This will help later when you are working pup on upland game.

If you start taking pup for walks from eight weeks on, she will prove herself well in the field by crashing through cover and not fearing any obstacles.

Rides

Take pup on rides. If you don't want her loose in the cab of the truck (never let the pup ride loose in the back of an open pickup truck!) or car, put her in the crate. Get her acclimated to riding so she looks forward to trips. If pup gets car-sick then start with short trips and gradually increase the distance. Don't feed her before traveling in case she gets ill.

Leash/Check Cord

I put dangling pieces of rope on the collars on my puppies at three weeks of age. The litter mates pull and tug on each other and get used to being pulled around without you being the bad guy. It's all a game. Put a nylon buckle-type collar on your pup right away so that she gets used to it being around her neck. Buy a lightweight six-foot lead to go with it or use a check cord. The sooner pup gets used to walking on a leash, the better off you'll be. Don't try and enforce any kind of heeling right now, just get the pup used to the restrictions the leash has. At first, let her drag the leash or check cord around loose. Most pups that haven't had rope collars on in the whelping box will jump and buck like a bronco when you first attach the lead to the collar and put tension on it. Ever so patiently kneel down and call the pup to you. She'll be confused but will look to you for comfort. Don't yank on the leash but use gentle pressure and lots of praise and food treats. Talk to the pup constantly telling her what a good girl she is as she follows you on the leash.

If pup constantly pulls on the leash and acts more like a sled dog than a spaniel there are two methods to try. One is to stop when pup pulls and just stand there, not saying anything. When pup comes to you, treat her. She will learn that pulling isn't productive.

If that doesn't work, use a little negativity - when she pulls, stop and yank on the rope and tell her, "Easy" and when she eases up on the rope, praise her by saying, "Good easy." You will worry about heeling later on. Right now you just want her to walk with you, not against you.

Starting Your Pup on Retrieves

Get an old white tube sock and tie knots in it. Kneel down and place pup between your legs. Hold pup by the chest and toss the sock down a hallway (close all the doors.) Keep in mind that the pup's eyesight is not very good at eight weeks so if the pup doesn't see the sock, pick it up and try again. The pup has no choice but to come straight back to you. If the pup won't pick up the sock, tease her with it by rubbing it back and forth on the floor right in front of her face and then throw it. *Limit to two or three good retrieves and quit with pup wanting more. **Always quit on a positive note** even if you have to back up and make the lesson easier.*

VERY IMPORTANT – When pup comes back to you with the sock or whatever in her mouth, do not grab it! Since you are still on the floor, with one hand support her chest and stop forward motion. With the other hand, push her rump down and tell her to 'sit'. If she drops the sock, don't worry about it. You are teaching the pup to sit to deliver her 'birds'. Most likely she is holding it and trying to escape. With one hand still on her rump, use the other hand to gently pry open her mouth while saying, "Drop." Teach the pup to hold now and it will be much easier to enforce the hold later.

Remember this when you move your retrieves to the yard. If pup comes back and drops her bumper, kick it with your foot and tell pup to *fetch it up*. Talk excitedly so pup gets fired up. Keep at it until pup sits and holds the bumper or bird. Get pup in habit of holding now and you will make your life much easier later on.

Even after she is ready to go outside to practice retrieves, give the pup two or three short lessons rather than one long one. If you try to give the pup retrieves until she is tired; she will lose her enthusiasm. If instead, you stop after no more than five retrieves, she will want more and the game is fun. If the pup doesn't want to retrieve, you can't force it. Try using something else as a retrieving dummy - a stuffed toy, a small paint roller, a tennis ball, or a bird wing.

Once you have tried teasing her and getting her excited and she still won't go, quit for the day. Dogs have off days just like we do. If the pup continues to ignore all attempts at retrieving it may be that she just doesn't have what it takes. It is much easier to check a dog that is headstrong than it is to force a dog to retrieve.

Before you give up on pup, ask yourself a few questions - Has the pup been loose all day and playing with the kids or another dog? If that is the case, she's probably tired. It may seem cruel to keep her penned up, but it's not. When you let the pup out, observe her. Is she is ready to work? Is she excited to see you? If pup still doesn't show enthusiasm, just back off and try again in a few weeks. Maybe she just needs maturity.

> ## The key to dog training is to always set the dog up for success.

The key to puppy training is limiting the amount of pressure you put on pup and making fetching a game rather than work. Worry about strict control later. Sure, maybe your pup is a genius and can do doubles, sits to the whistle and takes casts into heavy cover by the time he's seven months old. That's great *as long as pup is leading the way.*

Don't get discouraged if pup is not progressing as fast as your buddy's dog. When you get into competition over whose dog is smarter, the dogs lose in the long run because they are pushed past their abilities. Have fun with your puppy. You will have years of hunting enjoyment together as you both grow and learn.

The correct way to handle a puppy
when he returns with his bird or bumper.
• Don't grab the bird.
Put a hand on pup's chest and with the other
hand push his rump down to sit.
• Let pup hold the bird.
Gently pry open his mouth as you command pup to drop the bird.
• Don't worry if pup drops the bird.
You want him to get in the habit of coming back and sitting to deliver.

Chapter 6

Puppy Musts

Tools of the trade

✓   Collar, six-foot lead, two-foot check cord, and a twenty-five foot check cord

✓   Canvas puppy bumpers, rubber knobby bumpers, (Dokken dead fowl are optional but dogs really like them)

✓   Whistle and duck call

✓   Blank pistol, shotgun, blank shotgun shells (poppers)

✓   Birds

✓   Boat, Decoys

The *most* important thing to remember is that you and your pup *must* have fun. If it's not fun, why do it? Don't look at dog training as a chore, but rather as a series of challenges, ones that you and pup can master in your own time. Unless you compete in hunt tests, there are no *report cards*, only your journal entries to track pup's progress. Don't get uptight about the following list of things your puppy *must* learn to be a complete hunting companion. These are only guidelines. If pup does them by the time he's a year old rather than six months, that's okay too. I have found that pups that at least are introduced to all of the following items learn faster and easier than dogs whose owners wait until the dog is over a year old to start their training. I could say Puppy Shoulds but it just doesn't have the same ring to it.

You *must* get your pup in the water, on birds, with guns, through decoys and out of a boat before he is 6 months old. This is not to say the pup will be perfect - far from it. It only means that the pup has been introduced to all of these things and is comfortable with them. So many puppy owners have the idea that pup shouldn't get any *work* until he is 8-12 months of age. The thing they forget is that this is not work, it's fun! By the time pup is a year old he could be in the field bringing back your birds.

Last One in the Pond is a Rotten Egg!

You **must** get the pup in the water as soon as possible. It may take a bathtub or a kiddy pool with wading water, then adding a little more each day until the pup can swim. Lift him out of the water after a few seconds or have a platform or something he can climb onto to get out of the water. This is intended for an 8-12 week old pup but will work with older pups that have not been introduced to the water. Obviously you can't get enough water in a tub for a 6-month-old pup.

I have seen too many dogs come in for training at a year of age that can't swim. It can take months to resolve something that is so easy for a puppy. If it's warm enough, get the pup in the pond or stream. The easiest way is for you to walk in and let the pup follow. Wade in to where the water is only ankle deep. If you and the pup have bonded, he will follow you in. Encourage him. If he is getting wet, move into deeper water until pup is swimming. If he heads out for the next shore, gently reach under his belly and turn him back to shore. If the water temperature is still cold, take a towel with you and dry pup off so that his experience with water is positive.

Once the pup is comfortable swimming with you as the leader, take a bird wing or a small puppy bumper with you. Wade out just a little bit and toss the object only a foot or so into the water where the pup can still keep his feet on the ground. This gets him used to opening his mouth without worrying about sinking. Remember to keep the lessons short. Do only three or four retrieves and stop. Towel pup off if needed.

The next lesson, toss the wing or roller a little further. You get the idea.

NOTE: Keep in mind that you should always set the pup up for success, so think before you toss. You want the pup to get conditioned to go straight out and straight back. You don't want pup to run the bank in either direction. Stop before sending pup and see if he will be tempted to "square the bank" (cut corners and hit land instead of taking an angle back) on the return. So that pup doesn't do this, make sure your tosses are on the furthest point out into the water and that there isn't any temptation to cut corners. (See basic obedience on targeting *here* in Chapter 7.)

PROBLEM SOLVING: Older pup who won't go swimming. Be patient! Try wading in and seeing if the pup will follow. If the dog responds to food treats, use Goldfish crackers (they float) and let the pup go 'fishing'. I worked with a springer spaniel who loved to go fishing for Goldfish. He went from being afraid of the water - at six months of age - to leaping in for retrieves by the time he was eight months. Be prepared to get very wet since you will need to keep wading in further to encourage pup to swim.

If he is crazy about retrieving, use a canvas puppy bumper since they are easy for pup to grab. First toss the bumper in right at the shore. Don't worry about delivery, just swimming. Each time toss it a little further as long as you are getting pup to complete the retrieves.

PROBLEM SOLVING – POOR SWIMMER:

Some dogs just can't swim. It is not an automatic, instinctual behavior that can be called upon at any age. If you don't get your spaniel in the water as a pup you may have a lot of trouble later on. I worked with a one-year old Boykin spaniel who took over 3 months to learn that her rear end wasn't filled with lead. She would splash, splay-footed, all the way there and back, trying to touch bottom with her hind feet. She eventually got better coming back with the bumper/bird in her mouth, but as soon she got close to shore, that rump would drop and she'd splash her way in. The dog was definitely not comfortable in the water.

Birds, Birds, Birds!

You **must** get the pup on birds as soon as possible. I like my pups to retrieve their first whole, *dead* pigeon by 8 weeks of age. (You will probably not give pup a live bird until he is 5-6 months old so that the flapping wings don't spook him. The delivery may conclude by dragging the bird back, but a birdy pup will do the job.

With a new litter I introduce the pups to bird wings (kept frozen just for this purpose) as soon as they open their eyes. Let the puppies smell and grab the wing. Tease them with it. Don't leave it in the box instead, give the pups a chance at it two or three times a day.

At five to six weeks of age work each pup individually in the hallway. Keep in mind that the pup's eyesight is poor so your first throws will only be a foot or so away. Let the pup grab the wing. Do not pull the wing from the pup's mouth. If he has a firm grip on it, gently push his rump down to a sit and say, "Good hold." Push your fingers against his gums and gently pry his mouth open it while saying, "Drop." Teaching your pup to hold now can be invaluable later on in your training.

IMPORTANT: Make sure everyone in the family is consistent. Don't let the kids play fetch with the pup unless they can learn to handle the dog properly. Everything a pup does with a human is *training* to the pup. If he is allowed to make mistakes - or even praised for them - on one day and the rules change the next day, the pup will, through no fault of his own, become confused. For instance, the children squeal and encourage pup to play tug-o-war with a sock. Mom takes the pup out to train with a sock dummy and the pup is scolded for trying to play tug-o-war.

The secret to success is not letting the dog fail. Always be aware of what the consequences of your actions are now and in the future. If you grab at the pup and pull things out of his mouth he could start playing keep-away or dropping his bumpers/birds in anticipation.

PROBLEM SOLVING: If pup won't pick up the bird, try putting the bird in one of those tube socks and tie a knot in the end. The pup will relate to the hallway sock lessons and should pick the bird right up.

Some will lick at the bird but won't grab it. Pick the bird up, tease the pup by swishing the bird back and forth right under the pup's nose and then toss it a few feet. Talk excitedly to pup encouraging him to fetch it up. Keep doing this until pup picks the bird up and carries it a few feet. Praise the pup like crazy and quit this session while you are ahead.

Control

Once you move to the yard, you *must* put a check cord on pup. If you start out with a long line – about 25 feet – then you have something to grab if the pup decides to run the other direction with his bird. Make sure there are no knots in the loose end of the rope to tangle in brush.

Keep the line on him for the first 2–3 months. *Every* lesson starts with the check cord on the pup! Once he is reliable you can shorten the line to just long enough to drag the ground and for you to step on to keep pup steady.

Bang!

You **must** introduce the pup to gunfire carefully. A birdy pup won't do you much good if he bolts at the sound of a gun. Just as with children, don't treat pup with kid gloves. Make normal noises around the house. When you are in the kitchen, bang those pots and pans and if pup startles, don't make a fuss over him. Stop making noise and ignore him. When he settles down, make some more noise, just not as loud. He'll learn that the noise won't hurt him.

When the pup is eating, clap your hands loudly. If the pup startles, move away from him and try again. Once he is ignores the hand clapping, bang pots and pans together from a distance and gradually move closer. When he could care less about that, move to the yard with a .22 starter pistol. Have some help. Give the pup a couple of short retrieves to *prime* him and get him excited. You toss the bumper while your helper shoots the pistol from about 50 yards away. If the pup is so intent on the bird that he ignores the pistol, great! Move the helper closer gradually until the gunner is next to you. This may take one lesson or 10. Don't rush it!

Never shoot behind pup, always next to him or in front and to the side. Shooting behind pup can deafen him from the muzzle blast or worse case, pup could jump out and you might shoot your dog by mistake.

Once pup is used to the .22, use a shotgun, again with a helper. Remember to start off about 50 yards away. As pup relates *bang* to *bird* he will get excited about the gun and start looking for the bird.

PROBLEM SOLVING: If the pup becomes gun-shy you might be able to bring him around. As with most things, it's better not to get the problem than to try and solve it.

Walk with pup and clap your hands, at first softly, then louder taking to him and praising him as long as he's not cowering or showing fear. Millie Latimer, of Rock'n Creek Kennel, suggests the following: Once he is acclimated to hand clapping, use two blocks of wood (2x4 cut into pieces big enough to fit comfortably in your hands) and smack them together. Make noise around pup, always keeping an eye on him to see how he is reacting. If he reacts by cowering *do not* comfort him. If you make a fuss over him he will learn that cowering gets attention. Always relate the noise with good things - praise, food, or birds. If the pup accepts the wood blocks, then continue with the pots and pans and then work with the starter pistol and finally, the shotgun.

There are audio tape programs to help get pup over gun-shyness. If the methods outlined above don't work, see the Appendix for ordering information on gun-shy tapes developed by Steven Rafe in his Starfire Systems.

If a pup becomes gun-shy when previously there wasn't a problem, consider thunder and lightening as the source of the problem. If pup is near by when a tree or his kennel gets hit by lightening he will obviously be leery of loud bangs. Steven Rafe's, Starfire Noiseshyness Systems, has audio tapes to help with thunder storm fears as well.

Boats, Duck calls and Decoys

If you plan on hunting out of a boat and with decoys, these must be introduced to pup as well. If you are an avid duck hunter, pup needs to hear a duck call. It doesn't matter if you aren't a champion caller: the idea is getting pup used to the sound both from you and from the field. When you have an assistant or are training with a friend, use your duck calls as an attention getter (rather than 'hey hey'). During hunt tests, the judges usually have the bird boys blow on a duck call before launching the bird.

Start off with the boat on solid ground next to the water and teach pup to load up with the *kennel* command and *place* him on one of the seats or have a place for him on the deck or bottom of the boat. Introduce each new element as a separate lesson. First get pup to load into the boat and sit quietly in his place. Practice loading in and out of the boat when the boat is on shore. Then get out into wading water to work on loading in and out. The next step is to get into open water with you and pup in the boat. Next, take pup for a ride. Make sure you have a check cord on pup to keep him still and in case he tries to leap out of the boat.

When pup is comfortable in the boat, toss a bumper into the water and lift pup over the boat side and into the water. Be careful not to let the pup bang his knees or slip as he jumps out of the boat. Put plenty of non-skid tape all over the boat. Get pup to come straight back to you and let you lift him back into the boat. If pup wants to go around on land, move out into the water so that pup doesn't have any choice but to come back to you.

Take pup on fishing trips if it's not too hot so that he gets used to the motion of the boat and staying quietly in his *place*. If you are in the South, make sure you are in safe water – no alligators – where you can get pup used to going in and out of the boat.

Decoys are introduced on land. Place a few out in the yard and leave them there (as long as pup isn't loose later to chew them up). The idea is to get the pup used to walking around – and eventually, ignoring – the decoys. When training pup, toss the bumper/bird off to the side of the decoys. Get pup used to

Just Ducky's Johnny Walker

"Red" in a jon boat with a pair of Blackwater Decoys

"Red" on the place platform

going past the decoys without hesitation. Once he is doing that well, re-arrange the decoys in a wide spread so that pup has to go through them. Gradually condition pup so that he can go over and through the decoys without stopping to check them out.

Move to water. Put three or four decoys in the water. Toss the bumpers off to the side of the decoys so that pup has to swim past them. If it is a windy day the decoys will move and may spook pup. Keep that in mind and work a few yards away. As pup works past the decoys without hesitation, toss the bumper closer and eventually in the decoys. If possible, add to your spread and work the pup through a dozen decoys.

Finally, put the boat and decoys together. Take pup out and let him watch you toss out the decoys. Be careful here so that pup doesn't bail out of the boat and try to retrieve the dekes. This is why we are doing this now instead of at 4:00 in the morning on opening day.

Blow your duck call. Give pup a few retrieves through the decoys. Since pup has already been conditioned to gunfire, the last item to work into your training is to shoot a few blanks when you throw the bumper. If you have an assistant, ask the helper on shore blow a duck call and throw the bird or bumper while you shoot the gun. Pup now has all the basics for duck hunting. Keep practicing and by the time duck season rolls around, pup will be a regular pro at exiting the boat and swimming through decoys.

Let it Snow!
Just Ducky's Justimagine - "Maggie"
Edgefield, South Carolina - January, 2002

Just Ducky Kennel assistant trainer
Wayne Burnett working with Red on water marks

Chapter 7

Positive Reinforcement and Clicker training

Suggested Reading:

Don't Shoot the Dog! - by Karen Pryor – www.clickertraining.com
Culture Clash - by Jean Donaldson

Tools:
- ✓ (Training bench)
- ✓ Clicker, treats, nail pouch (for treats)
- ✓ Check cord and buckle collar
- ✓ Place Platform
- ✓ Four or five pieces of 1/2" PVC pipe cut into 10-inch lengths
- ✓ Canvas puppy bumper, knobby bumper, small plastic soda bottle, and a wooden dowel
- ✓ Bird

In a perfect world dogs would always come when called, never piddle on the floor, never chew up your favorite things and never need to be corrected. The fact is, sometimes you need to jerk on the rope, grab the pup and have a face-to-face talk, or smack him on the butt. Not very often, but just once in awhile to set the record straight in pup's mind and let him know you are the boss. Clicker training is a tool, just like the check cord and electronic collar are tools.

I am a strong advocate of clicker training for puppies and soft – tempered dogs for the beginning of their training. Once the dog has been conditioned to behaviors (like sit), the treats are gradually faded out until the dog rarely gets food and never hears a click again. There are purists who will be offended that I would put clicker training in with ear pinching for the force fetch ("conditioned retrieve" for the politically correct). If you have all the patience in the world and a dog that loves food and never leaves your side, then you could train this pup without ever raising your voice or hand. Most puppies will test you to see what they can get away with. Just like children, puppies need boundaries and rules set.

If you allow pup to dictate when he will come in, then he will only come in when he feels like it. Just because you have food in your hand doesn't automatically mean pup will come running. What if he's not hungry? What if the squirrel running around the tree is much more interesting and the squirrel runs into the road with pup following? You must be prepared to go to pup and grab him or his check cord and reel him in to you.

A super enthusiastic retrieving puppy has the drive to retrieve, no matter if you have prime rib in your pocket. Food treats will never replace the joy of fetching! The clicker training simply helps pup learn how to think and a thinking retriever is an amazing partner in the field. The clicker is a great tool in training the basics and so much easier on the dog than yanking and yelling.

I know what works and clicker training works. I used to be one of the old-school trainers – you know, the jerk and pull type. Pull and jerk on the dog until you get results. It works. But, it takes longer to train a dog that way and it's not any fun. Clicker training is fun.

Puppies love it. They have fun, you have fun, the pup learns. It is faster and much easier than the old jerk-and-pull methods of training. At 16 weeks, your pup can be sitting to voice command and a whistle, lying down, coming when called, and going to his kennel or *place* on command. I have found that the four-month old spaniel pup is at the ideal age to think and work for food. He is coordinated enough to walk and chew gum at the same time. You will thoroughly enjoy training pup, especially when pup learns the game and begins to exhibit all kinds of behaviors trying to make you 'click'. You can almost see the wheels turning in his head as he runs from the *place* platform, to the crate, to lying down, to sitting in front of you, looking for the right button to push.

The best part of all is that clicker trained dogs retain the information much better than dogs forced to respond. You can work the pup on the basics at four months of age and come back four months later to pick up where you left off. This isn't recommended, but it can be done. Read this book and **Don't Shoot the Dog** and start having fun with your pup.

The secret to clicker training is to be patient and to keep your mouth shut! You want the dog to show you a behavior (like sit) so that you can click and treat (C/T). The dog has to think about what made you click. At first, pup will be doing the *right* thing by accident. I can picture him looking at you and sitting just because he got tired of standing. You click and treat and walk a few steps away so that pup gets up to follow. Again, you are not speaking, and you may even be looking off to the horizon (with pup still in your side view). Pup is wagging his tail, jumping around and generally acting silly. He gets tired and sits to think about it. C/T. Get the picture? Eventually pup will learn that Sit means Click. When that happens, then you add the word, "Sit." Pup sits, you C/T and say, "Good sit." After you have several sits, say, "Sit" *before* clicking. Give a jackpot (a bunch of treats instead of just one) to pup when he sits on command. End of first lesson. The next lesson, start in the same area. When pup has the *sit* understood, move to another area of the yard. Then move again. Then, do it in the house. In the kennel. Anywhere you go, pup learns that *sit* means *sit*.

If you feel that clickers are definitely not macho, then use *good* in place of the clicker. Personally, I like the clicker better since it is crisp, quick, and consistent in tone. It not only cues the dog that he did *it* right, but it cues you as well. If you click too soon or too late you know it and can work on your timing.

Whether you use the clicker or your voice, learn to be patient. Give the pup time to elicit some behavior. He will – trust me – in order to make you click. This method is so much fun and so much faster than yanking pup into compliance. On top of all that, once learned, the behavior lasts!

The best part of all this clicker training is that once the behavior is learned you gradually remove the food and clicker. Instead of clicking and treating every time, you will click on a random schedule, say every 3rd or 5th time. Then you will click maybe once every 10 times. Just to keep pup on his toes, click twice in a row. If he does a super job, you will double or triple the treat (jackpot) a little like hitting the slot machines. After a jackpot you will stop the lesson on a very good note.

Eventually you will cease all treating except once in a blue moon. It is amazing how well pup retains his lessons just hoping that one of these times you will give him a treat. Why does a gambler continue to put money into slot machines? Because someday he'll be rewarded! The same goes with your pup.

Train only one behavior at a time. You can later work pup on multiple commands in one session, but when teaching a new command, concentrate on that one behavior until pup has it down pat. Teach sit. Then teach sit outside, inside, in the back yard, in the front yard, in your neighbors' yard. Then, teach down. And so on.

Treats – you can use store-bought treats like Obey® Training Treats or Bil-Jack® liver treats. Other options are just using the kibble you normally feed, chicken hot dogs, cheese, Cheerios®, home-cooked liver, or Goldfish® crackers. To keep pup on his toes, have several different treats in your pouch. A good ear rub, and a hearty, "Good Dog!' can also be used as positive reinforcers.

Getting Pup Conditioned to the Clicker

Before any training can begin, the pup has to learn what the clicker is and what it means. Get a pocketful of treats (use small plastic bags for the messy ones) and a clicker. I use a carpenter's nail pouch, although you can buy a fancy treat pouch at pet stores. Let pup loose in the yard. When pup comes to you of his own accord, don't say anything, just click and treat (C/T). Walk away, still not speaking. When pup follows, click and treat. Repeat until pup consistently looks to you for reinforcement. You will know pup understands the whole click and treat game when he starts offering different behaviors, like sitting or lying down.

Luring and Shaping Behaviors

Most of the commands you will teach pup will require that you show pup in steps what you want. To *shape* the down, for instance, you would *lure* the pup with treats (hidden in your palm) to lie down. At first if pup puts his front feet down you click and treat. Then, when pup puts his front feet and his head down you C/T. As pup learns you withhold the C/T until pup eventually lies down.

What you are doing is raising the standard and pup has to think about what makes you click. You can teach pup all kinds of parlor tricks as well as useful behaviors by shaping. For instance, if you want pup to ring a bell to tell you he needs to go outside the behavior can be shaped with a clicker and treats. With a bell hanging on the doorknob, start off by treating pup for simply touching the bell with his nose (you may need to rub some food on the bell to get pup to touch it at first). Click and treat and then open the door and say, "Good out-side." Gradually raise the standard until you only C/T when pup actually rings the bell.

Sit (to the Whistle)

Train your spaniel to sit to the whistle now and you will save a lot of headaches later when you are attempting blind retrieve training. Wait for the pup to sit. He will as he thinks about it and tries to get you to click. As soon as he sits, click and treat (C/T). When he figures out that sitting results in a C/T then and only then add the word, "Sit." Once he is sitting to command say, "Sit" and toot the whistle (one, single, short blast) - C/T for compliance. Gradually drop the word, *sit* and just toot the whistle then C/T when he sits. Alternate between the voice and the whistle until pup is solid on both. Move around the yard. Once he is solid at home, move to another yard. Then, move to another neighborhood. Add distractions like other dogs or children. You won't ask for steady (staying until sent for a bird or bumper) yet, just a good solid sit every time you toot your whistle or say, "Sit."

Advanced Sit

The ideal spaniel sits to the whistle, the voice command, the flush and the shot. Once pup is conditioned to sit to whistle and voice *and* **has been properly conditioned to gunfire**, move to the shot. If the pup has not been introduced to the gun, take the time to do this properly and come back to this later.

Have an assistant shoot a blank pistol while you toot the whistle immediately, C/T for compliance. Walk around the field repeating the exercise. If the pup is a few feet way from you, toss the treat to him or walk over to give it to him.

In another lesson have an assistant toss a bird, toot the whistle, and C/T for compliance. The key to solid sits is to do them over and over in all situations and different places. You can not do this too much as long as you keep it positive.

The last thing will be to combine the bird, the gun and the whistle. Live flyers are ideal, but if they are not feasible, use dead birds or bumpers. You will need to work pup with birds eventually, so start looking for a source for pigeons and ducks and put some in the freezer.

Down

Get pup to sit. With treat palmed in your hand, place your hand on the ground with the treat hidden in your loosely cupped palm. Most pups will drop down to try and get the treat. Click if you get a movement to lie down. You will gradually 'shape' the behavior by clicking only when the pup eventually is all the way down. Add the word, "Down" when pup is dropping completely.

Some stubborn dogs may need a little physical encouragement to lie down. Hook your hand in his collar (under his chin) and see if you can gently pull pup down. Another way is when pup has his front legs lowered and his butt in the air, simply push down on his rump. Be ready to C/T as soon as he drops all the way down.

Sit and Down 'Stays"

Instead of teaching *stay*, teach pup that sit means sit and down means down until you say otherwise. The way to do this is to delay the click and treat. At first you will only hesitate a second or two. Gradually lengthen the time until pup will sit or lie down until you release him on either his name or a click and treat.

Here is how to introduce the pup to *steady* (that is, to get the pup used to not moving until you release him). Begin by having the pup sit. When you put pup in a sit and he stays in place, you start moving around, just a side-step or backward step. Pup is used to you staying still so he will most likely move when you do. Be ready. Watch pup closely and as soon as you see a muscle twinge or a foot move, 'aaah!' him. When he sits back down, say, "Good sit" and move again. When pup is okay with you moving around, actually walk a full circle around pup. Don't allow him to move his feet. He may swivel his head to keep watching you; that's okay.

Once he has the sit (stay), repeat the exercise with the down.

Push-ups

When the pup is lying down, get him to sit. Use hand signals – with your arm straight down, the palm turned facing the dog, lift the hand up, bending your arm at the elbow (like a traffic cop.) If you need help, put a treat in your hand and wave it in the pup's nose to get him up. When he's sitting, C/T, and then get him back down and C/T. The hand signal for down is started with your hand up (palm facing dog, arm bent at elbow) and bring it straight down towards the ground. Over emphasize the hand signals at first, using treats to get pup to follow. You get the idea.

Why would you want to do this? Well, for one thing, it's a control issue. Say you are in a duck blind and pup gets bored and lies down on his own. That may be okay with you but what do you do if birds start flying and pup can't see the birds because he's lying down? If you could give him a quiet hand signal to sit up then pup could be ready to retrieve. As pup gets more experienced he will get his cues from the safety clicking off on your shotgun. In the mean time, teaching him to sit from the lying down position on command will do the trick. Another reason is that it's fun to show off to your friends. Third, some dogs will lie down to avoid further training. By teaching sit on command and raising up from a down, the pup learns that he can't pretend he doesn't know what sit means.

Targeting

You can use a target stick, but I usually prefer to use my hand as a target. Start by getting the pup to touch your hand and then click and treat (C/T). Once the pup has that down, start moving your hand and getting the pup to follow it and touch - C/T. When calling the pup *here* place your hand down, palm side toward the dog and C/T when the pup touches your palm.

The advantages to targeting your hand are several. First, you always have your hand with you. Second, you can get the pup to heel on either side by targeting the left or right hand. Third, you can get the pup to come straight back to you by targeting your hand. This will help later when you want the pup to maintain an angle on water retrieves, encouraging the straight back return rather than allowing the dog to square the bank (take a shortcut to dry land).

A target stick can be useful for training smaller breeds and young puppies because without the stick you'll have to walk around stooped over to get your hand low enough to be a target. A few training sessions spent stooping over can kill your back. You can buy a target stick or use something like a riding crop. Whether you use your hand or a target stick, the concept is the same, only you want to pup to touch the end of the stick instead of your hand. The target stick is easier to move around than your hand, which can help you to shape behaviors. If you want pup to heel around you simply move the stick around behind you with pup following. C/T in increments at first so that pup doesn't get discouraged. If pup makes it halfway around, click and treat. Step off and do it again. Gradually get pup to heel all the way around you and sit. NOTE: Do not treat if pup bites the target stick. You just want him to touch the stick with his nose.

Once the pup is targeting the stick you can use it for training other behaviors. Lead the pup to his place. Lead pup into the kennel. With pup targeting the stick or your hand, step off and teach the pup to heel.

Here

This is the big one. If the dog won't come when called you will have years of frustration. The trick is getting pup conditioned to come in no matter where he is or what else is going on. It has to be in pup's best interest to come when called. You have to make it worth his while to come in. Use your clicker and treats for coming when called.

Snap a long leash or check cord on pup and walk around the yard. Stop, and if pup is ignoring you, don't say anything but reel pup in, targeting your hand. When he touches, C/T and say, "good here." Wander around the yard (pup probably won't go far if you still have food and he hasn't eaten yet). Once pup understands *here* and comes in consistently, start treating on a random schedule, maybe once every three or four times, then twice in a row, then wait until the fifth *here*. Gradually you will stop treating except once in a blue moon.

Here is the one command takes the longest to fully learn. If you will be consistent and only say the word once, *and always expect and be ready to get compliance,* your life will be much easier in the long run. The trick is never allowing the dog to get away with not coming when called. No excuses.

Heel

Since pup has learned to target your hand or a target stick, advancing to the heel will be easy. When pup is walking by your side and touches your hand or the stick, C/T. If the pup is crazy about treats he will be prancing by your side begging for goodies. Take a few steps with pup along side and each time he targets your hand or the stick, C/T. Take a few more steps. When pup is walking at heel say, "Good heel" and C/T. Your aim is to be able to lift your hand up to your chest where pup can see it. Pup will still be targeting your hand and will also be watching you.

Take a few steps, and if pup is in the heel position – the dog's shoulder is even with your leg – stop, command *sit*, C/T. Repeat this several times. Each time you step off, go a few steps further as long as pup is in position. Once pup maintains the position, add the word, *heel*. Remember to praise pup when he gets it right. I use a lot of *good heels* and *good sits* along the way.

Teach pup to heel on both sides. This comes in handy mostly in hunt test/field trial situations where you want to block the dog from taking a bad angle entry in the water or if you need to help the dog take a better line for marked and blind retrieves. It can also be useful when working two dogs if you have each one heeling on either side. If you normally heel your dog on the left, use the command, *heel right* to get pup on the other side. Vice versa for right side heeling, training pup to *heel left*. (If you are a left handed shooter you will want to heel pup on your right side away from the gun.)

Kennel

You can teach your pup that kennel means get into the crate, the car, the boat, the blind, or the kennel run. It's easy. Just toss some treats into the crate and when pup steps inside, click and treat. Some pups pick this up very fast. Others will try your patience, so be cool. After you have shown pup what you want and he will go into the crate with food, wait him out. If you have a pup that really likes treats he will eventually go inside. If he is reluctant, then gently put him in the crate, saying "Kennel," click and treat compliance.

Once pup is going inside with you next to the crate, start stepping back a few steps and sending pup from a distance. Eventually you will be able to amaze your friends when pup will run and kennel in his crate from across the yard or room.

Repeat the process in the kennel run and anywhere else you want the pup to load.

Word of caution: Do not ask your dog to jump in and out of a truck, especially a young dog, since he could severely injure himself.

Place

The *place* command comes in handy in several ways. One way is in the house. Teach pup that his place is his dog bed. When you are having supper or when company comes over, tell pup to go to his *place*. No more begging or jumping on the guests!

Another way the place command is handy is in the field. Suppose you want pup to sit outside the duck blind so that he can see the birds fly and (hopefully) fall? Or, suppose you are in a duck boat and want pup to sit on a certain seat or on a platform? If he knows *place* it's easy to transfer one *place* to another.

You must start with a place that pup can delineate from his surroundings. It can be a dog bed or a boat cushion or a platform. Let's start off with a platform. You can build a portable one easily with pressure-treated 1x2's and plywood. I added hinges to mine so that it would fold and carry easily. It only has to be big enough for pup to sit – about two feet by two feet is plenty for the average spaniel.

If pup doesn't want to step on the *place*, you can shape the behavior. Lure pup to the place with treats. When he puts his foot on it, C/T. Once he gets the idea of this new game, raise the standard and wait for both front feet to get on the platform. Then all four feet. Each time when you click and treat, step away with *okay* to release pup from the platform. Get him to step off the platform, wait a few seconds and see if pup goes back for more treats. Then, require pup to sit (you say, "Sit") before clicking and treating. Pup should do all of this in the first lesson. Finally, when pup is going to the place consistently, add the word, "Place."

In the next lesson go back to the same area and work pup on his place. Once he goes to the platform on command, move away and send pup from a few feet away. You may have to take a step towards the platform until he gets the idea. Gradually work further away until pup will run from 20 or 30 yards away to his place.

When you need to transfer the command to a different *place*, go back the basics and lure pup to the new place like the boat seat or his dog bed. It will be much easier with every new location you teach pup. My pups learn that the passenger seat of my truck is their place. The drivers' seat is mine.

To get pup to sit and stay in his place, delay the C/T, releasing pup on his name or *okay*. Once the pup is going to his place and staying, start adding distractions. Have a check cord on pup in case he breaks. Toss your hat in the air. If pup moves, 'ahhh'! him and put him back on his platform. This is the first step in training pup to learn to be steady.

When pup holds the sit with the hat, try a bumper. Step on the check cord to make sure pup doesn't break. Pick up the bumper yourself if pup does break. When pup gets a good retrieve, have him deliver to his place.

To really test the pup, have a bird you can toss. After pup is conditioned to the gun, shoot and throw a bird. Always have pup bring the retrieved item back to the place and deliver to hand. If you are clicking and treating at all, you should only do so for delivery to your hand.

Later, when you start training on blind retrieves (the dog doesn't see a bird fall so the hunter gives pup directions to the bird with whistle and arm signals) you can use the place platform for pup to sit on at the pitchers' mound. It gives pup a definite place to work from during the baseball drills. There will be much more on blind retrieves later in this book.

Look (at Me)

If the dog won't make eye contact with you, how are you going to train him? This is really important when you move to blind retrieves. Sit the dog facing you and wave a tidbit of food in front of his nose. Bring it up toward your face and as the dog's gaze moves up and makes eye contact, say, "Good look" and then C/T

Repeat several times, extending the length of time before treating. If pup looks away say, "Look at me" and C/T for compliance.

Anticipation

To have fun with the pup set up a little area with a place platform and a dog crate. The pup will start anticipating your commands and will run into the crate and jump on the platform, all aiming to make you click that thing. This is a good way to teach the pup not to jump the gun, but instead to wait for your command. If you say, kennel and he goes to the place, wait him out to see if he corrects himself. Use the infamous 'aaah'! noise that all mothers know. Most men have to be taught the sound but women have been using it for years keeping their children out of harm's way. When he goes to the crate and gets in it, C/T. You want to get pup to the point where he waits to see what you will ask for instead of anticipating.

Hold/Fetch

The only drawback to clicker training I have found is that if the pup has too much clicker training before he understands the hold command (and sometimes even if) he will drop his birds to get a treat. So, we will put pup on the bench and teach the hold. The trick is to have something easy for pup to grab and still have a hand free to click and treat.

I discussed this with my good friend and bird dog trainer, Mark Fulmer of Sarahsetter Kennel, in Aiken, South Carolina. Mark also utilizes the clicker in his training and seminars. He introduced clicker training to me several years ago and for that I am very grateful.

Mark came up with the idea of using 10-inch pieces of ½- inch PVC pipe for teaching the hold. It's easy for young and old spaniels to grab and you can put plenty of them in your pocket for times when pup spits them out. You can slip an end of the pipe on your finger so that pup grabs the pipe instead of your hand.

Have some chicken hot dogs (or other really yummy food) for treats. Rub the hot dogs on the pipe. When pup licks the pipe, C/T. Don't say anything to pup. Be Patient! Gradually raise the standard until pup has to bite the pipe to get the reward. If pup won't bite, put a piece of hot dog in the end of the pipe. You may have to put the pipe in pup's mouth a couple of times to show him what you want. Don't force it. Gently put the pipe in pup's mouth and immediately click and treat. Then, delay the C/T so that pup holds the pipe. In order for pup to hold and get conditioned to continue holding until you release, only click after you say, "Drop." When pup is grabbing the pipe, say, "Good fetch." We are mainly concerned with the hold right now and will gladly take (and treat) any offered behaviors like the fetch. If the pup continues to fetch, don't C/T until you command, "Drop." If you click for the fetch, pup will spit out the pipe for the treat.

With the pipe in his mouth, delay the click until pup takes a step and continues to hold. Tell him, "Good hold" and have him sit. Be prepared with your hand to stop pup from spitting out the pipe when he sits. With pup sitting, use the command, "Drop," and C/T. Next, get pup to walk with the pipe. Then, C/T only when pup is sitting *and* holding. Just keep raising the standard until pup is grabbing the pipe and carrying it the length of the bench, sitting and holding until you say, "Drop."

This isn't going to happen in one lesson. For the first lesson, get the pup to lick the pipe. If you get him to grab it, great! Jackpot and quit! Next lesson, see if you can't get the pup to grab the pipe and hold it for a second or two. Get several fetch and holds and quit. If pup regresses, don't worry. Make the lesson easier so that you get a positive response, and then quit for now. With lots of love and patience, pup *will* get the idea. Don't rush it.

Once pup is holding, walk around the bench and work pup from both sides. While pup is holding, walk a few feet away but stay close enough to reach in and correct pup if he spits the pipe out.

While pup is holding, reach down as if to take the pipe. Instead of taking the pipe, reach down lower and pat pup's chest. This teaches pup that every time your hand drops toward his mouth is not a cue to drop his birds. Talk to pup and tell him what a good dog he is. Lift your hand back up and then command the *drop*.

The ultimate goal here is to get the pup to fetch off the bench and later, off the ground. Take one piece of PVC pipe and add 'T' joints to each end so that it will stand elevated on the bench to make it easier for pup to grab. Hold the modified pipe in your hand and when pup grabs it, say, "Good fetch." Have pup carry the pipe down the bench and sit. Tell him to drop and C/T. Repeat. Get to where pup fetches on command and doesn't drop until told to do so.

Pup is used to taking it out of your hand and now you want him to pick it up without your help. Put the pipe on the bench with your hand next to it. As pup learns the game he will pick up the pipe off the bench without your hand nearby.

Sit the pup and walk a few feet away command, "Fetch" and if pup is confused, tap the pipe on the bench to encourage pup to come on. You want pup to grab the pipe on the move. Get pup to walk up and down the bench with the pipe and only C/T the drop. Finally, sit pup at one end and place the pipe a few feet away, command the pup to fetch. If pup isn't sure what to do, shorten the distance and go back to encouraging pup by tapping the pipe on the bench.

Once pup has the PVC pipe down pat, it's time to work in other items. Use a canvas puppy dummy, a one-liter soda bottle, a knobby bumper, a wooden dowel, and of course, a bird. Avoid using sticks since pup may offer to bring you sticks to play with instead of concentrating on work. Do each item separately until pup is solid on each. Then switch between items until pup will hold and carry anything you ask him to on the bench.

Don't be discouraged if pup doesn't pick the fetch up right away. Clicker training can demand tons of patience! You can't rush the dog into behaviors, he has to figure them out for himself. You can show him and lure and shape him into performing but eventually he has to understand what you want. The only way to do that is to let him make mistakes and be prompt with your clicks when he gets it right.

Distractions

Once pup is holding and carrying, you need to add distractions. Have other dogs running around, or have children or another adult standing nearby and talking to you. You can really test pup's grip by waving the food treats in his nose. If he drops the pipe, 'ahhh' him, replace the pipe and repeat until pup understands he doesn't drop until commanded to do so.

You're Grounded

Okay, pup has this *hold* thing figured out on the bench. Now, we move to the ground. Don't expect pup to be perfect right off the bat. You have to start all over. The good news is that this time it won't take as long to get the message across.

With pup on a check cord, step on the cord so you have both hands free. The rope keeps pup from taking off with his trophy. Sit pup down and offer him the PVC pipe. If he grabs it, tell him, "Good fetch" and "Hold." If the pup doesn't grab the pipe, place it in his mouth and tell him to hold. You will do everything you did on the bench, only now you're on the ground. When pup is carrying the pipe and delivering it to hand, you will use the other items – the bumper, bird, etc.

No Training Bench?

If you don't have a training bench you can still teach pup. The bench makes it much easier on you and pup, you since you don't have to bend over and you have pup's undivided attention. You can use a tailgate of a pickup truck but be careful that pup doesn't fall or jump off. And of course, you can work pup on the ground. The best part of that is you don't have to deal with repeating the lessons learned on the bench. The down side is the stress on your back.

You can easily make a bench and it doesn't have to be fancy. Ideally it is 16 feet long, made out of pressure treated lumber and just tall enough for you to handle pup comfortably. You don't want to have to reach up to work with your dog or bend over. It doesn't have to be freestanding so you can work all the way around it. Look around your home to see if you can attach a bench to the porch or a section of the house. It doesn't have to be 16 feet long. It does need a cable or pipe overhead to attach a chain to hold the dog.

Troubleshooting: The *Really* Soft Dog

The overly soft dog needs special care. If you find your pup displaying submissive behavior it is important that you work on his confidence. *Never* reward the pup for belly crawling or for lying down when you call him. Do *not* coddle and baby him. It will only make the behavior worse. Use treats and the clicker to encourage pup to come to you and sit. C/T only when the pup complies. If the pup just lies there and won't even get up, walk away and turn your back on him. Do not say anything. When he comes to you (and he will, be patient) keep your back turned to pup, without eye contact he should sit. C/T, praise him and do it again. Keep the lessons short and as frequent as possible.

All training on the really soft dog must be positive. You even have to be careful about yelling at him unless it's a life-threatening situation (i.e. dog running out in the road). Be careful, but remember not to baby him. Talk to him in normal, excited tones. If you baby him he will only get worse.

Dogs Who Aren't Motivated by Food

If you have a pup that could care less about food, try some other treat. I trained one dog who lived for bumpers. So, when he obeyed a command, I tossed him a bumper. This can get pretty bulky so see if you can't find a small stuffed toy or squishy ball that you can put in your pocket.

I had another dog that lived to go swimming. When he did his lesson well, he got to jump in the water and go after a bumper. That was his reward. No clicks needed.

You may find that your pup has no interest in treats when it comes to retrieving. That's great! His reward is the retrieve. Save the clicker and the treats for the obedience work.

Boykin spaniel, Story's Cocoa Break
at 6 months learning to hold on the training bench

Chapter 8

Gentle Hold Method

Tools:
- ✓ (Training bench)
- ✓ Clicker, treats, nail pouch (for treats)
- ✓ Check cord and buckle collar
- ✓ Leather work glove
- ✓ Four or five pieces of 1/2" PVC pipe cut into 10-inch lengths
- ✓ Canvas puppy bumper, knobby bumper, small plastic soda bottle, wooden dowel
- ✓ Bird

If you start training your pup using a clicker and treats, and didn't work on the hold before everything else, you will probably get a pup that drops his birds so that food can go where the bird was. If you are lucky you will get a pup that loves to carry things around in his mouth and is reluctant to give them up. Not hard-mouthed, just 'sticky'. If you are really lucky you will get an obsessive/compulsive dog that can't pass by a bumper on the ground without picking it up and carrying it around. These pups are so much easier to work with than pups who spit everything out. Remember that everything the pup does is learned behavior – you may have inadvertently taught pup to drop his birds by grabbing at the bumpers when he was just starting out.

When dropping bumpers becomes a problem, I do gentle hold training on the bench at about five months of age. Pup has been in training and is conditioned to sit on voice and whistle commands, obeys *place*, *kennel*, and will come to you when called. You teach the hold first since you want the pup to hold his birds until you command to drop, even if he's soaking wet coming out of the pond. With a birdy pup you may only need to teach the hold since the drive to retrieve is so strong.

If you are not utilizing the clicker and treats in your training you can still do all of the exercises explained. The only difference is that you will use verbal praise and it may take longer to get results. See Chapter 7 on clicker training for teaching the fetch with positive reinforcement.

At five months of age pup is still teething so you don't want to use anything too large or too hard for him to hold. I like to use the small puppy canvas bumpers and 10-inch long pieces of ½ – inch PVC pipe. First, get pup acclimated to the bench. Lift him up and talk sweet, petting him and letting him know it's okay. Snap the chain to his collar so he can't jump off. It may take a few days just to get pup comfortable walking back and forth. Use the clicker and treats until the pup is happy being in this elevated position.

Once you have pup easily accepting the bench it's time to start holding. Get a heavy leather work glove on one hand. Sit pup and get him cornered against the post so he can't get away. If you have a restraining chain on the post, use it as well as the top chain. (If you are working pup on the ground, have a long enough check cord that you can loop over your shoulder and step on the end.) Gently open pup's mouth and put your gloved hand in his mouth with your thumb resting on his chin. He will probably buck and twist and try anything to get that thing out of his mouth. Be patient and gentle, but do ***not*** let him spit your hand out. Once he has quieted down, say, "Drop" and remove your hand. Repeat until he accepts the gloved hand without fighting. When pup is holding say, "Good hold." End of first lesson.

When pup is accepting the gloved hand, move to the PVC pipe. It's small and easy to grip (and easy to spit out.) Have several pieces ready and put them in your pocket so that when pup spits one out you are ready to replace it with another. Praise pup with lots of "Good hold" encouragement. When pup is holding without your hand propping his mouth, say, "Drop" and C/T. Pup is going to learn that he doesn't get a treat until he hears the word *drop*. You can really test pup's resolve by waving a treat in front of his nose while he's holding the pipe or bumper. If he drops the pipe, 'aaah'! him and put it back in pup's mouth. Pup will learn that he doesn't drop until commanded to do so.

The next part can be tricky: you will need to be quick with your hands! When the pup is sitting and holding the pipe for at least a minute and releasing on *drop*, it's time to get the pup to carry. Have one hand under his chin, lightly cupping the muzzle to catch the pipe if pup spits it out. The other hand will gently pull pup towards you so that pup walks with the pipe in his mouth. Be patient and be ready with extra pieces of PVC in case pup spits it out. Repeat these lessons every day, twice a day if possible, until pup will hold and carry anything you ask him to; a bumper, a plastic soda bottle, a wooden dowel or a bird.

HRCH UH Curlee Gurlee

with her upland clip that makes it easy to

keep the cockleburrs under control

Chapter 9

Conditioned Retrieve

The conditioned retrieve, formally known as force-fetch training, consists of teaching your dog to fetch anything you ask, anytime you ask, without fail. The conditioned retrieve will **not** make a retriever out of a dog who has no desire to retrieve. It will make a so-so dog more reliable in the field. It will make a great spaniel a finished retriever.

There are several ways to teach the dog to fetch, most of them incorporate avoidance of pain on the dog's part: the toe-hitch, the ear pinch and the electric collar. Clicker training is the only positive reinforcement method and if your dog is a good candidate for clicker training, read Chapter 7 and use it.

This book is about training spaniels and how they are different temperamentally than Labrador retrievers. Most spaniels can't handle the pressure of being forced to do anything. The spaniel pup wants you to show him and then ask nicely if he'll please comply. When you try to scold, hit, yank on the collar, or pinch the ear of your pup, he'll most likely do one of two things: roll over on his back or bite you. Well, maybe both. So, how do you go about training pup? Do not lose your temper. Stay as unemotional as possible when starting the conditioned retrieve. You have to learn how to read your dog and know when to apply more pressure to force the issue and when to back off. There is no set formula as each dog is an individual. It's a fine line, I know. If you stop at the wrong time, the dog will learn he can get away with not doing what he is told. Yet, if you push too hard, too fast, pup may quit all together.

Pup is holding and carrying bumpers and birds, so now it's time to fetch it up. Count your blessings if the pup does this naturally. Equally blessed are the owners of dogs who only take a minimum of pressure to get the point across. I have trained a handful of Boykins who only needed to have their ear pinched five to ten times to get the message. On the flip side, I have also trained a handful of Boykins who tried my patience for *months* before finally getting the point. If you are not comfortable putting any pressure on your pup and don't have the patience to work through this with clicker training, send him to a professional trainer. It's better to not start the conditioned retrieve than to start it and not follow through to completion.

Keep notes in your journal to keep track of exactly how pup is progressing. It can be important to remember if pup took twenty tries one day to fetch, only five tries the next day, yet it took twenty-five tries the third day. If there is inconsistency in your training methods it will show up in the journal. Why did pup revert? Did you do something different? Were there distractions that weren't there the day before?

Timing is Everything

When do you start the conditioned retrieve? It all depends on your dog and his or her temperament. If pup is crazy about retrieving you may never need it. Teaching the hold may be all you need. If hunt tests interest you, and pup is a slow maturing dog, you may want to wait until he is at least a year old. Keep him excited. Give him plenty of birds and work on conditioning the hold. If you decide to start the program, do ***not*** give your pup any retrieves until the conditioned retrieve is completed (exceptions are explained later). Do not take pup hunting until the conditioned retrieve is completed. And I mean completed! If you shoot a bird for a pup that is not solid on his retrieves you will lose all that you have accomplished up to that point. If you shoot a bird for the pup and he doesn't retrieve, what are you going to do? If you don't enforce the fetch you will be going backwards in your training. If you do force the fetch in the field you run the risk of turning pup off of birds.

If you plan on entering in hunt tests you will need to go through the entire conditioned retrieve so that pup picks up and delivers anything you ask him to. The birds at some hunt tests are less than desirable, especially in the hot months when the same birds are used the second day of the trial. The dog has to be conditioned to retrieve birds that are not fit for the table to say the least. The *meat* dog won't have this to contend with, as all his game will be fresh.

Start off the conditioned retrieve with either PVC pipe or a wooden dowel. You will move to bumpers and birds once pup is solid on fetching non-birdy stuff. There is less chance of pup turning off of retrieving bumpers and birds this way.

Okay, ready? Have pup sit. Hook your four fingers of the hand closest to the pup under pup's collar and reach for the ear flap. Pinch the ear between the nail of your thumb and your forefinger. The reason you have hooked your fingers under the collar is to have control to keep pup from biting you to avoid the pain in his ear. Say, "Fetch" one time. As soon as pup opens his mouth put the PVC pipe in and release his ear immediately. Say, "Good fetch." Let him sit and hold the pipe for a few seconds and then ask for a release with *drop*.

To keep pup's spirits up, click and treat. Some dogs will be upset and not want food during these lessons. Use a lot of praise. Remember to keep your voice neutral. The idea is that the ear pressure is no big deal. It stops when pup opens his mouth. Repeat. If pup fights you, hook him up on the bench so that he can't move his head to avoid the pressure. If you can't get pup to open his mouth, use ear pressure with the one hand and pry his mouth open with the other hand to place the pipe in pup's mouth. It takes a little dexterity, but with practice, you'll get the hang of it. Using the pieces of PVC pipe makes this easier since they are small in diameter. Say, "Fetch" as you put the pipe in the pup's mouth. Try and get one fetch without ear pressure. Praise the heck out of pup when you do and quit for that lesson.

Don't Get Emotional

The key to the conditioned retrieve is to keep from showing any emotions. The dog learns that when he opens his mouth, the ear pinch pressure stops. Period.

Once pup is fetching on command, have pup walk and carry the pipe, sit and deliver with the *drop* command. Some dogs need a lot of coaxing to get them to understand that they can walk and carry something at the same time. You may need to hold your hand under his chin and help support the pipe to make sure pup doesn't spit it out. You may have to push his rump down for the sit. Have your other hand near his mouth in case he drops the pipe to sit. Whatever it takes, remain calm. Don't get mad if pup won't sit or tries to drop the pipe. Relax your standards on everything except the fetch and hold. He'll put it all together eventually. Repeat. *Always* end on a positive note even if you have to back up and make the lesson easier. Walk him down the bench and have him sit and release on command. Treat and quit for that lesson.

There may come a time where you both are ready to quit. Pup just won't get the idea and you are getting frustrated. Don't stop now (unless you are going to lose your temper.) One of the indicators that pup understands the lessons is when he doesn't want to give the object back. When this happens you are almost there. To get pup to release, place your finger inside his mouth and press on his tongue. Or, gently pry his mouth open and treat for the *drop*.

After pup has begun to confidently fetch the pipe out of your hand, have him fetch a wooden dowel. A soda bottle. A bumper. A bird. Work up to each gradually by having pup fetch it out of your hand. Encourage him and even place the item in his mouth until he gets the idea. Alternate between items until pup will fetch anything out of your hand on command.

When you want pup to pick up items off the bench first start off with the pipe. Add a 't' to each end of the PVC pipe to make a dumbbell that will sit elevated on the bench. This makes it easier for pup to pick it up. Tap the bench with the pipe and get pup moving and excited. Hook your hand through his collar and say, "Fetch." If he fetches, praise him like crazy. If he doesn't apply ear pressure until he does, then praise him like crazy! Repeat until pup will fetch without ear pressure. Treat and quit.

Next lesson, start off tapping the bench then set the pipe down and move your hand before pup fetches. If he hesitates, move your hand near the pipe as you apply ear pressure. He needs to learn that your hand does not need to be touching the pipe. When pup is fetching the pipe off the bench without ear pressure, move to the wooden dowel, then the soda bottle, next a bumper, and last, a bird.

The final step on the bench is to get pup to sit while you place an item on the other end of the bench. When you command the fetch, pup shouldn't hesitate to go and pick up the pipe or bird. If he does, apply ear pressure until he can't wait to put something in his mouth. If pup is still reluctant, go back to tapping the pipe on the bench and getting pup excited. Get him to fetch on the move, then lightly restrain him with one hand while you place the pipe down with the other. Command the fetch while being prepared to use ear pressure if needed. Keeping pup moving also helps to keep him more relaxed. Talk to pup in an excited voice to show him how much fun all this really is. Once he understands that he is going to fetch whether he feels like it or not, he will start feeling like it since life is so much nicer when he does.

Once pup will fetch everything you ask while on the bench it's time to move to the ground.

I have trained a few spaniels who start off doing great on the bench and then regress. This often happens if the dog learns to hate the bench lessons. You will know you are in trouble if you have to drag pup over to the bench to start training. Instead of fetching on command (which the pup was doing) the dog requires constant force. In this case, it sometimes helps to go ahead and put the dog on the ground and start over from there. Get the pup to hold at a sit and then come to you, holding the pipe or bumper. Enforce the hold rather than the fetch. You have to learn to read your dog to decide which way to go with the training. The dog will still have to complete the force-fetch training, only now you will move to the ground before pup totally shuts down on you. Ease up on pup and use as much positive reinforcement as possible.

On the ground, use a check cord on pup so he can't run off. Start all over from the beginning. Have pup sit and fetch the PVC pipe from your hand. Then have him carry it at heel. Have him sit while you walk away from him (you are holding or stepping on the check cord) and then call him to you. If he holds and sits to deliver, after the *drop* praise the heck out of him! Command pup to fetch the pipe off the ground. If he doesn't comply, pinch his ear until he does. Once he is fetching the pipe, go to the wooden dowel then the soda bottle, then the bumper, then the bird. You get the idea. This isn't going to happen in one lesson. If pup is a quick study he may fetch the pipe in one lesson. The next lesson get him to fetch the pipe and the dowel. Next lesson, go for the pipe, dowel, bottle and bumper. The best way to work pup through the conditioned retrieve is to schedule two 15 minute lessons each day. A lesson should never last longer than 30 minutes. If pup grasps a concept quickly, don't push him too fast. Remember to give pup a refresher course at the beginning of each session so that you are both starting on the same page. Just because pup fetches the pipe and the dowel one day doesn't mean he'll do it the next day. And, if you wait a day or two between lessons, start off from scratch: tell pup to fetch from your hand and if he doesn't, apply ear pressure. Dogs do not reason like people – if he doesn't obey your command, chances are he doesn't understand what you want, so show him.

While you are working pup on short retrieves with the check cord, have pup heel and carry the bumper around the yard. If he drops the bumper, command the fetch and if he doesn't comply, grab his collar, pinch his ear as you lead him to the bumper. He has to understand that he doesn't drop until you tell him to.

Okay, pup is fetching off the ground, carrying objects at heel and delivering to hand. Now, get pup to leave your side and fetch when you toss something. You throw the dowel a few feet and pup runs toward it and keeps on running without picking it up. Since you have the end of the check cord in your hand, reel him in and with your hand through his collar, pinch his ear until he fetches. You don't have the check cord in your hand? Okay, go to pup and get the check cord and using ear pressure all the way to the dowel, get pup to fetch it up. Remember, no emotions. Don't yell, "FETCH!" at the top of your lungs. The only emotions are the happy, excited tones pup hears when he does it right.

Some dogs will flip over, lie down, do anything to avoid the pressure. With your hand firmly hooked in his collar, flip him back over or lift him up to fetch. Do all of this without emotion. Just don't let him dictate how the lessons are going.

If you have one of those spaniels that simply hate any kind of correction you have to find the balance between when to apply pressure and when to let up. A lot of spaniels need a combination of both. If pup is reluctant to accept the pressure of the forcing you will need to *happy him up* by relaxing the standards. Try clicker training first. If that's not your 'bag' or pup isn't interested in treats, spend at least two weeks on the bench, pinching the ear and getting pup to fetch. Don't stop the training unless pup is showing signs of shutting down and quitting completely. You may just need to put pup in his run and leave the lessons alone for a week or two maybe even a month. Go to happy stuff like walks and positive obedience work.

Some dogs respond to fun retrieves. If you are using the PVC pipe then some pups will still retrieve bumpers. If you are using hard rubber bumpers for the force fetch, then switch to canvas bumpers or better yet, birds. Get pup off the bench and go into the yard with a bird. If pup refuses to fetch, tease him with the bird and get him excited. Get him to grab the bird. Best case scenario is pup fetching the bird and having fun. Give him a couple of retrieves and quit. If pup won't fetch the bird sit him down and gently place the bird in his mouth and have him hold it. Get him to carry it towards you for a few feet, command the drop and quit.

If the pup is crazy about water, give him a break and let him retrieve in the water. This can be dangerous if pup leaps in the water, goes to the bumper and refuses to pick it up! You have two options. If the pup refuses to *fetch* after swimming into the water, you can A) go swimming with pup and make him fetch the bumper or B) toss another bumper closer to shore where you can control the fetch. Either way you are probably going to get wet so unless you know pup will retrieve in water, don't throw it or be prepared to go swimming.

You may get pup excited again by using jealousy. Get another dog to work with. Make sure the two dogs won't fight over the same bumper. Send the other dog out for the bumper while holding your dog steady. Then have someone hold the other dog and see if your dog will fetch. If he won't, turn the other dog loose and let him fetch it up, giving the other dog all the praise.

You will have to find the right combination of pressure for your dog. There is a point where you have to work through the problem. There is also a point where you have to step back and give the pup some space.

If you have a pup who is advancing through the conditioned retrieve beautifully, the last step is to get pup to fetch in the water. Most pups love the water so the only trick is to teach pup to hold and deliver his bumpers *before* he shakes. The pup's natural inclination when coming out of the water is to drop the bumper or bird in order to shake off. If the pup won't be entered in hunt tests you may not care how clean the delivery is. You are happy as long as pup picks up the bird after he shakes off and brings it to you.

If pup is not crazy about the water, you will need to use ear pressure in the water as well. This means either waders or you just get wet. Keep the check cord on pup so you maintain control. Start off at the edge of the water and gradually move further out until pup has to swim to fetch. Train pup the same as on land until pup will fetch reliably on command.

Start off at the edge of the water so that you can reach down to guide pup in and be ready to correct pup if he drops the bumper. Remind pup to hold as he comes out of the water. Keep your eyes on pup and if he starts to shake, *aaah*! him, tell him to sit, and take the bumper from him. As pup learns this concept, move back further on land.

Just Ducky's Justmyluck - "Lucky"

Chapter 10

STEADY

Pup needs to be steady to wing and shot. If you have been restraining him all along then this will be easier than if the pup that has been allowed to break and run on every throw. Keep the check cord on pup even after you feel he is steady. Just in case. It is always better to have the check cord on and not need it than to need it and not have it.

Sit pup and hold the check cord in one hand. Be prepared in case pup breaks but leave slack in the line. Toss the bumper and be ready to grab the line with both hands. If pup sits, wait two seconds (one thousand one, one thousand two, said to yourself) and then call his name to send him. If pup breaks, you are ready with both hands on the rope and are braced for the inevitable end of the line jolt. (With a small dog it isn't too hard to bring pup to a standstill by simply waiting for pup to reach the end of his rope. With a large dog you may want to wear gloves to reduce rope burn.) At the same time you are bracing to stop the dog, your whistle is in your mouth and you hit one blast for *sit*! Best-case scenario, pup sits and waits for your next command. What is more likely to happen is that pup will continue charging to the bird until he is stopped by the rope's end. Heel pup back to you and sit him down. If he will sit and stay, walk out to the bumper and pick it up yourself. If he won't, walk him out at heel. Do *not* let him get the bumper if he breaks. He must learn that he only goes when his name is called and he doesn't get the bumper if he breaks.

Once pup is steady on bumpers, move to dead birds. Repeat the exercise until pup is solid. Then add the shotgun with the birds. If possible, next move to live birds. Shackle them so they can't fly away unless you have a call-back pen. Tease pup with the bird and let it fly. You will need an extra pair of hands for the next step - add the shotgun with the live birds. It's pretty difficult (not to mention unsafe) to handle pup, shotgun and the bird at the same time! NOTE: I don't believe in 'fun' bumpers (pup racing to fetch before he is released) as I feel it encourages breaking . The dog sits and is restrained, either by check cord or command, for every retrieve.

English springer spaniel
Buzz Lightyear Space Ranger MH
photo by Ron Klimes

Chapter 11
Marked Retrieves

Pup has been retrieving well with you throwing the bumpers or birds yourself. It is time to get pup going further than 30 yards and that means you need a helper. Pup needs to start looking out for the birds and not expect them to always come 'out of your arm.'

Start in an area where your thrower stays and throws in the same area and you can back up with pup to lengthen out the distances. Also, start with white bumpers and short cover so that pup sees the bird/bumper in the air and all the way to the ground. At about 30 yards away from the thrower, sit pup and hold on to the check cord – held so that there isn't any slack in the line. If pup is rambunctious and needs more restraint, kneel down and put pup between your knees and hold his collar. Signal the helper to yell, 'hey hey' or blow a duck call to get pup's attention and throw the bumper. Let the bumper hit the ground and wait two seconds before sending pup on his name.

Sometimes the pup will want to take the bumper to the thrower. Before this happens, be ready. Have the thrower instructed not to look at the pup, in fact, turn away so that the pup sees the thrower's back. Make sure all the bumpers are in a bag off the ground or in the thrower's vest so that pup doesn't get the opportunity to drop one bumper and pick up another. Whistle and encourage your pup to come back to you. If needed, use the check cord and guide him back in.

American Water spaniel
SHR UH Waterway's Dax WD

If the pup does well at 30 yards, back up 10 yards and try again. The thrower should try to put every bumper in the same area. As long as pup is successful, keep backing up until pup is going about 50 yards, straight there and back.

If pup is not returning straight back, use the check cord to get him in. Do not stretch pup out for longer retrieves if he is not going straight there and back. Get one or two good retrieves and stop. Remember to always end on a positive note.

Once pup is consistently retrieving in one area, move to another but still use short cover and white bumpers. Each time you move to a different field start off with an easy mark and gradually stretch it out longer.

When pup is marking perfectly in short cover it's time to move to moderate cover. Instead of short mowed grass, find a field where the bumper isn't immediately visible but the cover is sparse enough so that when pup is within a few yards of it he can see it. Again, you will start short – about 30 yards – and gradually lengthen the distances. Move around the field so that pup is starting from a different spot. Then, both you and the assistant move to where pup gets different views and marks. Keep stretching out the distances as long as pup is successful.

If you get to where pup hunts short, encourage him to *hunt it up*. If the pup starts to come back in, have the assistant **run** out, pick up the bumper, yell, 'hey hey' and *when he has the pup's attention*, toss the bumper straight up so that it lands in the original spot. Do not have the assistant run out if the pup is actively hunting in the area of the fall (where the bumper fell). Also, if pup keeps getting lost make the marks easier so that he doesn't start looking to the assistant for help. Do not move to heavier cover until pup is perfect in moderate cover.

Now you can move pup to heavier cover and different terrain. Everything is done gradually, 'show and tell' training. When you move to heavy cover, shorten the marks so that pup is successful. When you move to a hill, start off with short marks uphill. Keep in mind that wind and terrain will alter pup's path. Cross-winds will 'push' him sideways, hills will cause him to take angles. In order to compensate for the terrain and teach pup to take a straight line *no matter what*, do it in steps. Always start off as easy as possible. Put your thrower at the maximum distance and you move pup close for the first retrieve. As pup is successful, back up. If you back up too far, move closer again. You get the picture.

The same goes when you change cover. Let's say you are working on a field where there is standing corn with rows cut for dove hunting. Or, there is a road running through the field. Cover changes can throw a dog off line. Work through them gradually so that pup learns that no matter where he is, he takes a straight line to the bird and back.

Once pup is solid on different cover and terrain with white bumpers, change to orange bumpers and birds. Remember to start off easy and gradually make the distances further and the cover heavier. Increase the distances as long as pup is successful and move up to make it easier if pup is having difficulties.

Work pup in as many different terrains as possible. Find a cornfield where there are plowed rows. Work pup in fields where he has one or two cover changes (from grass to corn to mowed paths, etc.). Some fields have roads cutting through them. Use all cover changes possible. Work him on angles through the cover. Each time you take pup to a new area remember to shorten up the marks until pup is proficient. You are training pup, not testing him.

Three generations of UKC/HRC titled Boykin spaniels

left to right:

HRCH UH Curlee Gurlee

HR Just Ducky's Justasample (Sammy)

SHR Just Ducky's Justdoit (Nike)

HR Just Ducky's Tourbillion

Rock'n Creek Bird Boy x HR Just Ducky Justasample

Chapter 12

Following the Gun

Get pup used to you sitting or kneeling next to him. Most pups will get all excited when you drop to their level so do a few retrieves to get pup looking out and concentrating on his work. Handle an empty shotgun and at first simply point the gun at the arc of the throw. Have your helper move to different areas of the field. Line pup up straight towards the thrower and as the bumper or bird is thrown you follow the path with the shotgun. Make some of the throws off to the left and right so you both swing away and into the pup's path.

When pup is comfortable with you swinging the gun and is marking the fall, start using ammo. Blank popper loads are the safest. If you have to use live loads, be very careful of the location of your helper (and don't shoot your bumpers.) Pup *must* have already been introduced to the gun and be comfortable with the noise.

Have someone hold pup since he is going to get very excited when the gun goes off. You don't want pup to learn to break on the shot. Make the throws in short cover so pup has a good look at the bumper all the way to the ground. Depending on the area you may get an echo and pup will swing his head to the sound and not see the bumper fall. If this is the case, have your other assistant shoot the gun and you actually hold the pup's head so that he watches the fall. Don't release pup and let him run all over if he doesn't mark the bumper. Have your helper pick it up and try again. Pup will learn that he needs to stay focused on the shotgun and where it is pointing in order to get the bird.

To get pup looking out and not just looking for a thrower, set up in a wooded area. You handle the pup and the shotgun and have your helper move around, hiding behind trees or brush so pup doesn't see him. At first, have the helper yell, 'hey, hey' or blow on a duck call to get pup's attention. Once pup learns to follow the gun, have the helper throw without making any noise. You tell the pup to 'watch' to get him looking out and prepared for a bird to fall. If pup is having a hard time grasping the concept, have the thrower set up to toss the bumper in a direction so that you have to swing the gun past pup's head to shoot. If you are heeling pup on the right, have the assistant throw to your right so pup learns to swing with the gun.

The best way to teach pup this is in the field (assuming you are a better shot than I am.) Pup will learn quickly that 'bang means bird' and if he pays attention to which way the gun is pointing, he will get to fetch a bird.

Chapter 13
Water Marks

When introducing pup to water marks there are a few things to keep in mind. You want pup to go straight to the bumper/bird and come straight back. While this is not as important for the *meat* dog, sometimes you'd rather he didn't go out of his way to find land to make the retrieve. That means going straight there and coming straight back. Some dogs, once they learn that they can get to the bird faster on land, will avoid the water like the plague. This can cause a problem if the cover is particularly heavy or if the bird is crippled and moves from the original spot.

The key to water marks is you, the trainer, thinking before throwing. Plan out your training sessions before you toss the first bumper. Set yourself up near the middle of the pond or at least in an area where the pup is not tempted to hit land too soon (such as a point of land sticking out.) If there is a point, heel pup out on that point. Find clear water - without lily pads and/or cattails - to start and get pup's confidence up.

Toss the bumper straight out in front of you. The pup should come straight back. Good. Gradually lengthen the marks until pup is swimming 50 or 60 yards.

Angle Entries

Once pup is going straight out and back you will start teaching him to hold a line even if it means taking an angle. Toss a bumper about five feet to the left (or right) and send pup. Since you have taught pup to target your hand use it to lure pup straight back to you.

You will gradually change the angle of entry/delivery, but the pup should maintain a straight line to and from the bumper. Don't go further than 45 degrees for now. If he tries to *square the bank* – cut his swim short and hit land then come back via terra firma vs. water – scold pup, take the bumper from him and toss it back in the water. Keep doing this until pup gets the idea. Back up and make it easier by reducing the angle. Remember, show and tell. Put pup up. The next time, start from the beginning and work the opposite side so that pup learns to swim the angles from both directions. If pup doesn't seem to get the idea, try using a long check cord and reel pup in. For short retrieves you can use a Flexi-lead, the longest one available is about 30 feet.

Water/Land/Water

To keep pup from running the bank when the bird drops close to the opposite shore you need to have some help. If you don't have help, have an angel on your shoulder for good luck or a really long check cord.

Keeping in mind that you have worked pup on *here* you will try to get pup to return by water. Find a pond with a corner where you can hand throw the bumper all the way across to hit land on the opposite shore. Start far down the bank where the pup has to swim and the bumper lands at least 30-40 yards from the opposite shore. Work pup on easy retrieves, emphasizing the turn-around in water. Gradually move down the bank towards the narrow corner. What you want is to *show* pup what you expect. As you move to a tighter mark (closer to the other bank) toss the bumper closer to land. Do **not** put the bumper on land if you can help it! If your throw is off and goes all the way over, hold your breath and pray that pup makes the turn and comes straight back. This is where the helper is needed. If the pup tries to come back by land, have your assistant block the way around, take the bumper out of pup's mouth (just take it, don't ask for a sit), toss it back into the water (towards you) while you encourage pup to come *here*. Repeat. If pup doesn't get the idea, back down the bank and make it easier on pup. Quit for the day on a positive retrieve and try again tomorrow.

Once pup is going in the water, retrieving the bumper on land and coming back by water, it's time to send pup from further back on land. Instead of sending pup right from the shoreline, move back in five to ten yard increments until pup is running to the water, swimming to the opposite shore, running 20 to 30 yards on land to retrieve the bumper, and coming straight back.

Angle/Water/Land/Water

You can make water retrieves as easy or as hard as you want. If you plan on running pup in hunt tests you want to show pup every possible angle and entry as you can.

To teach pup to take an angle into the water from way back on land you will start from the shoreline. Refresh pup's memory with easy throws. Use your hand for pup to target. If he is successful, back up on land about five yards at a time. As long as pup maintains the angle to and from the bumper you are doing great. You want pup to take off from 40 or 50 yards from the waters' edge, hit the water, keep swimming across the pond, go on land, pick up the bumper and come straight back to you. Don't rush it. Take your time and do this right. If you push pup too fast he will get confused and figure it's just easier to go by land. Try to always set pup up for success!

As with land marks, once pup is proficient on one pond, move to another. Find ponds with different cover and flooded timber if you have access to some and start all over again.

Note: If you are training in the winter, please take into consideration the water temperature. Don't push pup to do too many retrieves in frigid water or he may just refuse to go at all. Who can blame a dog for trying to find dry land when the water is freezing cold?

Just Ducky's Justacrooner - "Bing"

Chapter 14
Advanced Steady

Okay, now pup is waiting until his name is called before retrieving. We are going to add a little extra to test him. When you are ready to send pup, be ready with the check cord, and instead of saying his name say, "Dog." He will most likely break since he is conditioned to go as soon as you say anything. Hit the sit whistle and heel him back. Pick up the bumper and try again. And again. Once he is solid on *dog*, try using other names or any gibberish that you can come up with. I use all the names of all my other dogs, as well as fruit and peanut butter. You can make it really tough by using words that start with the same letter as the dogs' name – for "Sammy" I may say sugar, stone, silly, etc. The dog learns he does not leave your side until his name is called. This will come in handy in several situations – afield when the birds are flying, shotguns are blasting, and hunters all send their dog on *back* except you. Your dog stays by your side until he is sent by name. The main other situation is when honoring another dog, especially in a hunt test scenario.

Steady with even Tougher Distractions

Once your pup has been introduced to, and is competent on his marked retrieves, go out with your hunting buddy and her dog. Find a field or pond where you can walk around comfortably, throwing up to 100-yard marks. You

95

each heel your dogs, with bumpers in hand, going in opposite directions. Start off at about 50 yards. You throw for your buddy's dog and your dog sits quietly at heel while the retrieve is made. Then it's your dog's turn. Move around the field or pond and give each other several marks from different angles. You can even throw doubles (if you have already taught pup to count to two) by throwing the bumpers in opposite directions. This works with three or four handlers as well as two. It teaches the dog patience as well as honoring and steady. With the extra handlers you can make the session tougher with doubles and triples.

Once pup accepts the other dog retrieving 'his' birds, it's time to work almost side by side and do actual honoring. Keep the check cord on pup to make sure he won't break. Take turns with the other dog each making retrieves. Mix it up so that maybe your dog gets two or three single retrieves and then has to honor the other dog working two doubles. You don't want pup anticipating when he will get a turn. When pup understands the concept start off a session with pup having to honor straight off the truck. Later in the training, have him honor *after* he gets his marks. Pup needs to learn that no matter how exciting this game is he doesn't get a bird until you tell him he gets a bird.

Chapter 15
Modified Doubles (Diversions)

You are out hunting and shoot a bird. As pup heads back with his bird you shoot another one. Pup drops the first bird (which happens to be crippled) and goes after the second. That is called a *switch*. Bad dog! What happens if the first bird retrieved *is* a cripple and when pup drops it, the bird takes off, never to be seen again?

What pup needs to learn is that he always brings back one bird before getting another one. You will start teaching this on land so you can run out and correct pup when he makes a mistake. This exercise also gets pup thinking about a second bird and is a great way to introduce doubles.

Sit pup at heel and toss one bumper out for him. Send pup and let him return and heel. Do **not** take the bumper from him. Have him hold it as you throw another bumper. If pup spits out the bumper in his mouth, 'aaah' him and tell him to fetch. Don't let him fetch the other bumper in the yard. After you ask pup to drop the first bumper ask him, "Where's the bird?" When he looks out into the yard at the bumper, send him. When he comes back, repeat the exercise until pup will hold the first bumper until you ask for it and fetch the other one on command. This exercise not only reinforces the *hold* but sets pup up for doubles later on.

The next lesson, do one or two repeats of the first lesson. Now you are going to toss a bumper (at least 45 degrees away from pup's path) as pup is coming back. He is likely to spit out the bumper and run for the other one. If this happens, stop him and make him fetch the first bumper. Use lots of praise to get pup coming back in. Line him up for the second bumper. Make sure you are using short cover so pup can easily see the bumper since he will be confused at first. Repeat until pup gets the idea.

When pup has it figured out on land, move to water and start all over. It should be easier for pup to grasp the concept on water, and pup can't swim as fast as he can run so you can make corrections easier. Make sure you throw the bumpers on wide angles away from pup at first so he isn't as tempted to switch.

The hard part comes when you work with birds. Pup gets a lot more excited with birds than bumpers, so be prepared to stop pup if he tries to switch birds. The final test is adding the shotgun with the birds and shoot the bird when pup is returning with a bird in his mouth.

Note: All of this isn't going to happen overnight or even in a week. It may take a month of lessons to teach pup to deliver one bird before going after another. With all of pup's training, when teaching a new concept, only train that one lesson until pup understands. Once he has grasped the idea, then mix in other concepts. For example, when pup is steady and doing doubles *and* understands diversions, throw a diversion as pup returns from the last bird down on a double. Don't take for granted that pup will remember all of his lessons - we all need refresher courses once in awhile. Relax the standards when you first start combining two or more factors.

Chapter 16
Doubles

When pup understands that he gets one bird at a time you are ready to see if pup can count to two. Advancing to doubles will also help getting pup steadier on singles since he will be waiting for the second bird to fall.

Using very short cover and white bumpers, sit pup down and throw one bumper out at about a 45-degree angle. When pup comes back in have him sit and hold the bumper he just fetched while you throw the other bumper in the same spot. Take the other bumper from pup's mouth and throw it 45 degrees in the opposite direction. Send pup and he should go after the last bumper down. Heel him around and sit him facing the second bumper. Ask him, "Where's your bird?" and when he looks out where it is, send him. If he is confused and doesn't remember then move pup up closer at heel until he sees the bumper. Try again until pup counts to two and remembers the second bumper.

Start off with short marks and make sure they are wide enough apart that pup isn't tempted to switch and go to another bird or in the area where he's already picked up a bird. This usually happens when pup hunts the area and can't find the bird. Instead of continuing the hunt, he figures he'll just go find the other bird instead. If pup does switch before he picks up the bird, yell "*No!*" at him and run out if needed to stop him from picking up the bird. It is very important to stop pup from switching if you are going to run him in hunt tests since he can be failed for switching.

As pup gets better at simple doubles, stretch them out longer and move to moderate cover. When pup is hitting every mark, change to orange bumpers or move to heavy cover or cover changes. As you progress pup through the tougher marks, (to keep pup from getting lost) start off with a long single and then make that same single the memory bird (throw it first so pup has to remember where it was).

Later, when you want to teach pup to count to three, you will build on the marks just like you did for doubles. Have the double launched or thrown for pup and the next time, do the same double and you throw a third bird/ bumper from the line (where you and pup are standing). Once pup learns to count to three on land, build your triples in water.

CAUTION: Throw singles for pup most of the time, in all different cover, up and down hills, building on them and gradually making them longer and harder. If you only throw doubles and triples, pup will start head swinging (look away before the bird hits the ground) in anticipation of the next mark. This can cause pup to forget the memory birds since he really didn't get a good look at them.

For gun dogs, I know I rarely (if ever) hit a double in the field and have never shot a triple! Of course if you are hunting with friends, there is a chance that two or three birds will be in the water or the field at one time.

Chapter 17
Extra Curricular Activities

Walk-ups

The scenario here is that you are walking up on a pond full of Woodies. As you approach several birds jump up and you take a shot at a drake. Pup bolts off into the water and flushes the rest of the birds. Problem is, you missed!

Pup needs to be steady to wing and shot. He must learn that he doesn't leave your side until you send him – no matter how exciting life is. To teach pup about walk-ups you will need some help. Have one person ready and hiding behind a tree so pup doesn't see him. He will throw the bird/bumper out in your path. Have another person handle the shotgun so you can be ready with the check cord if pup breaks.

As you walk, talk to pup. I use the word, *easy* to indicate that we are slowing up just in case a bird flies out. This helps in hunt test situations to key pup that a walk-up is in progress and he should be on his toes. The gunner says, "Bird in the field" or "There goes one" to cue the thrower. The gunner shoots at the arc of the throw. Brace yourself in case pup breaks. If he even jumps out a few feet, heel him back before sending him. If he breaks, scold pup and try again, this time with the end of the check cord in your hands and someone else doing the shooting for you. Don't let pup creep out in front of you. Do **not** let pup get the bird if he's not *completely* steady.

Problem Solving

Once pup understands the concept there is a little trick you can do if pup still breaks. You handle the shotgun and have your helper carry a riding crop. If pup jumps out, the helper has to be quick and smack pup on the rump with the crop. Wear long pants in case the helper misses the dog and hits you by mistake!

Obstacle Course

Ever since your dog's puppyhood you and your pupil have been going for walks through the woods and pup has learned that nothing gets in his path that can't be climbed over, gone under or through. We are going to build on that by setting up an obstacle course for pup. If you don't plan on campaigning your dog in hunt tests you may not feel this is necessary. You are right. But, it is fun and the dog enjoys the game.

Use a little imagination. Finding the right area may take some time. I set one up in my front yard. There are two four-foot logs at the starting point, spaced about two feet apart. Forty yards away is a brush pile. Thirty yards from the brush pile is a sturdy bent tree limb that has been anchored so that the dogs have to go under the 'knee'. The finished dogs start off going between the logs, over the brush pile and under the knee – fetch the bumper and return straight back. Each obstacle is shown to the dog individually then combined one at a time. Both marks and blind retrieves are utilized on the course.

Most dogs learn well by example. I know you have heard stories about the Boykin who watched his mother or uncle work or learned how to fetch via the video classroom. If it were only that easy! Seriously, dogs do learn some things by watching. If you want pup to go over the brush pile, you lead him over the brush pile. Then you sit him right in front of the brush pile and toss the bumper a few feet over it. Send pup. He is so close to the pile that he hasn't any real choice but to go over it. Whistle him back over. If he tries to go around, stop him and coax him straight back. Gradually back up and toss the bumper further, insisting on straight over and back.

Next, set up two chairs or find two trees pup can go between. Walk the pup through the trees. Set him right in front of the trees and toss the bumper between. Send pup and encourage straight returns. You get the idea. Once pup has the trees and the brush pile down individually, set up a mark so that pup has to maintain a straight line and do both, go over the brush pile and through the trees, retrieve and return straight to you. Add on more obstacles if you like. Move to other areas. Consider sand piles or hills, gullies, ditches (be careful and examine areas well so pup doesn't step into a hole or ditch and hurt himself), streams, creek beds, etc. **Every time you take pup to a new area with new obstacles, show him first what you expect.**

Dax and the author leaving the holding blind on their way to begin a hunt test series

Photo by Pat Trichter-Deeley

The Invisible Line (remote marks)

You are sitting in your duck blind and pup can't see a thing. You want to place pup outside the blind so he can mark the fall and you still have control. In order to do this you must work pup from a distance. The place platform conditions the dog perfectly for this scenario. The place platform can be anything that the dog can delineate from the surroundings. It can be an old shirt of your, a piece of carpet, or a wooden platform like the one I use. It should be easily portable so you can take it with you wherever you hunt.

Place the dog on his platform and leave his side with the *sit* command. Move 10 yards away and toss a bumper. You can ask pup to deliver back to the platform but it isn't necessary as long as pup brings the bird to hand. Change around and throw the bumper from both sides and with you further away from your dog. Imagine different scenarios where you and pup will be hunting and set up similar training sessions. Maybe you and pup will be hunting on the edge of a pond. You may want to stay hidden behind a tree, yet pup needs to be out in front so he can watch the birds fall. If this is the case, start working pup where he is off to one side and you are behind him. If you are behind your dog, however, always be aware of how close you are to your dog before you shoot so that the muzzle blast doesn't deafen him.

Platform diving (flooded timber)

There may come a time, either in a hunting situation or a hunt test, when you need to work your pup off of a platform. You may be hunting in flooded timber where you are wearing waders and in order for pup to see the birds fall he needs to be elevated above the water. If you have worked pup off of a platform for the *place* this will be easy. If you have worked pup off of a dock so he learns to jump into the water, that's even better.

As with the remote sits pup doesn't have to deliver on the platform, just as long as he delivers the bird to hand.

The Holding Blind

If you are going to play the hunt test game you need to get pup used to the holding blind. The blind is usually made up of three poles that can be pushed (or hammered) into the ground with camouflage material stretched in between. The blind is used out in the field to help hide the bird boys and wingers as well as being a holding station when you are waiting your turn to run your dog.

Get your pup used to the blinds so that he doesn't get spooked if the wind flaps the material right about the same time he gets close to the bird. Also, work pup waiting behind the blind and heeling to the line to work. At hunt tests you and pup will be required to wait behind the blind right before it's your turn to compete. Dogs sense your nervousness and often lose all memory of what heel and sit means. Once pup has experienced his first hunt test he will most likely get very excited about the prospect of another. Chances are good that pup will 'forget' his manners, especially his line manners!

Sometimes pup will be asked to sit outside the blind while you are behind it. There will be times when you are hunting and pup won't be able to see the birds unless he is outside the blind and staying steady. Working on remote sits and marks will come in handy both in the field and at hunt tests.

Sit and Down (You, not the dog)

Dove hunting will most likely find you sitting on a dove stool with pup by your side. Some open field goose hunting may require you to actually lie down so that birds don't spook and flare away from you. Work pup a little with you lying down (unless you will find yourself in a lot of goose fields) and a lot with you shooting from the dove stool or bucket.

Mock Trials

If you are going to play the hunt test game, then you and your hunting buddies/ training partners should set up mock trials. Get as many people together as possible to try and fool the pups into believing this is the real thing. Use birds, holding blinds, guns, poppers, decoys, boats, judges chairs, bird boys, and everything else you might see at a hunt test. These mock trials are the best way to correct problems that only show up at hunt tests. Some dogs who normally heel perfectly and sit to every whistle, may be out of control heeling on a walk-up and ignore your whistles on blinds during competitions. If the dog gets the idea that you *can* correct him at hunt tests he may change his attitude.

Curlee going over the brush pile in an obstacle course

Chapter 18
Blind Retrieves

Blind retrieves will be the most time consuming part and the hardest part of training your spaniel to be a finished retriever. The dog **has** to trust you, to believe in you, to take your word for the fact that the bird really is 30 yards away to the left instead of 45 yards to the right where there is tons of bird scent. You will do drills. You will do confidence/sight blinds. You will do them in the backyard. You will do them down the road. You will do them in this pond and that pond. You will do them *"Sam I Am,"* until you and pup are working as a team. You will make it easy. You will make it fun. You will not test pup, but train him. You will not get fed up and quit because it can take six months to earn pup's trust. Even then you are not through. By the time pup is three or four years old and you both have hours upon hours of training and a couple of hunting seasons under your belts, then you can start to relax and enjoy the fruit of your labors.

I recommend the book, <u>*Training Retrievers to Handle*</u> by D.L. and Ann Walters. It is a *must have* in any retriever owner library. What I will discuss here are the basics and some of the finer points that I have learned over the years regarding the spaniel temperament and blind retrieves. You will need a dozen white bumpers and a dozen orange bumpers. You can do this with less, it will just mean more walking for you to plant the blinds while working pup on the drills.

Okay, pup is steady. Pup is sitting to the whistle. Pup has to be sitting to the whistle. If he isn't, work on that before you go further than the baseball drill. Pup has to sit immediately when you toot for *sit*. Work pup on a check cord and when you toot, pop the cord and stop pup in his tracks. If he keeps coming, move toward him with your arm up-raised, and tell him to *sit*. Go back to using treats and when pup sits to the whistle, toss him a treat. Walk around the yard and spend ten to fifteen minutes just reinforcing the sit. No matter where pup is in the yard, when you hit the whistle, his butt hits the ground.

> You don't have to wait until the pup is solid on doubles to start teaching pup to handle. As soon as pup is steady you can start playing baseball with him.

Now it's time to start teaching pup to take directions. It's easy and if you make it a game, pup will enjoy it. If you make it like a drill, he will hate it. So why not make it fun?

Back!

Sit pup at the 'pitcher's mound' (you can use your place platform to make it easier for pup to remain steady) and walk away about 20 yards so that you are facing him. Toss a white bumper over his head towards 'second base'. He will look and he may break. Stop him and sit him back down. If he picked up the bumper, take it from him without fanfare and toss it back over his head again. Once he is sitting (and probably looking at the bumper) wait until he looks at you. Tell him, "Look at me" (See Clicker Training chapter) until you get eye contact. Once he looks at you, raise your hand straight up, palm flat facing the dog, and say, "Back." He may sit and look at you. Step towards him and raise your arm up again and say, "Back." Have pup deliver the bumper to you and sit him back on the place platform. Repeat no more than 10 times a session.

Over!

Once pup understands *back*, it's time to go *over*. You can get fancy and say *left* and *right* but it gets confusing – whose right, yours or the dogs'? Just stick to *over* and keep it simple.

Again, you will place the pup on the pitchers' mound. Toss a bumper to your right. When pup is looking at you, stretch your arm straight out to the right side and say, "Over." Overs are a much easier concept since pup can see the bumper being thrown with out having to turn his body. Once pup understands *over* to the right, work on going to the left.

Now you are going to ask pup to take directions from you and not just go after the last bumper down. Sit pup on his platform and toss one over his head and one to each side. Now, toss one more over his head so that this is the last one he sees thrown. Give him a *back*. He should go back and pick it up. If he tries to go over stop him and sit him back down in his place before sending him back. When he delivers to hand, place him back on his spot and send him back again. After he gets back and is in position for the next cast, toss one bumper over his head and one to the right (or left). Pup will not get to fetch the one thrown behind him since we now want him to learn to go to each side. Cast him over and when he gets back, cast him over to the same side again. Now do the other side. Quit for this lesson. I like to walk to another area and toss a few marks for the dog to reward him for doing the drills. Try not to throw the marks in the same area you are doing the baseball drills.

Once pup has this drill down pat, toss the bumpers out as before but don't throw the extra bumper. Cast pup to whichever bumper you want. When pup returns, toss that bumper back where it came from and cast pup a different direction. He will want to go the one you just tossed so be prepared to stop him and re-cast him. If he doesn't get the idea, toss another bumper in the direction you want pup to go. When you get pup taking a cast in each direction, stop and give him a few marks. Repeat this lesson as many times as needed until pup will sit and wait for you to tell him which way to go.

Next time you go out to train, put the bumpers in place before you have pup with you. And now you will put three or four bumpers in each location. Each time you will be raising the standard. When pup is consistently taking every cast you give him, change to orange bumpers. If pup can't see the bumper he may be confused at first so you may have to toss an orange bumper in the direction you are casting pup to get him going.

Every time you change areas and especially when you move to heavier cover, back up and start all over again. Let pup see you throw out the bumpers and build his confidence by starting off easy. As you and pup progress and you start to work as a team, it will take less time to advance to *cold* blinds (bumpers or birds planted before pup gets out of the truck). Eventually pup will learn to trust you, but that trust takes a lot of time and a lot of drills.

Walking Baseball

While all these drills are going on you are also continuing to reinforce pup for sitting to the whistle. With pup running around the yard, toot for a sit (and toss a treat for compliance).

Now you are going to play a version of walking baseball. With pup running in the yard, toot for a sit. When pup sits, toss a bumper. Pup ***must*** be steady for this to work. Cast pup to whichever direction the bumper went. When pup delivers the bird to hand, release him and do it again. Each time toss it a different direction. You can do this drill before or after the more tedious drills. Pup will love it since this exercise more like marked retrieves.

Once pup is taking the casts, add another bumper. Toss one for pup and send him. When he is going out, toss a white one in a different direction. When he comes back, sit him down and walk away about 20 yards and toss the bumper you just got back in a different direction. Pup will be used to going after the one you just threw but you want him to fetch the other one. If he tries for the wrong one, sit him down and re-cast him. Work with pup, using lots of body English to get pup to move in the right direction.

This exercise is a good one to get pup casting into the water. Sit pup down near the bank and toss a bumper in the water. Cast the pup whichever way will take him straight into the water. This is especially good for starting to teach pup to take a *back* in the water. Sit pup down with his back to the pond and stand back about 10 yards. Toss one over pup's head and cast him *back*. Since he already knows it on land he shouldn't have any problems.

Lining Drills

At the same time you are doing the baseball drill you can also incorporate lining drills. This will give you a break from the baseball and get pup starting to take a straight line towards the blind.

In a different area of the field or yard walk pup at heel and toss about 10 bumpers on the ground where he can easily see them. I like to put the bumpers in a straight line about two or three yards apart. You are going to put the bumpers in the same area every day. Turn and heel pup back about 30 yards. Face the pile of bumpers and tell pup, "Dead bird." When he is locked in on the bumpers, say, "Good" and then release pup on his name. Each time pup is successful, move back another 10 yards. Next time out start out at 50 yards away. If pup seems confused, move up until he sees the bumpers, when he locks in, tell him, "Good" and send him on his name. Keep moving back until pup is taking a straight line for 100 yards. Repeat this exercise until pup will take the line on the first cast.

The next lesson, place the bumpers before you take pup out. He should remember where the pile is. Move so that you are sending pup on different angles to the same pile. When pup is proficient it's time to move to another area. When you introduce pup to a new area remember to shorten the distances and gradually increase it until pup is charging straight for a hundred yards without hesitation.

As you move to moderate cover where pup can't see the bumpers, make sure you mark the area with surveyors tape so you know where the pile is. Walk pup out with you and toss the bumpers for him to see where they are. When you turn and send pup, and he is confused as to where the bumpers are, keep moving closer until he can see the bumpers. When the cover is too heavy to see the pile, sit pup, walk out and toss one of the bumpers in the air, walk back to pup and send him. At first it will be easier if you have some landmark for pup to focus on - a tree or bush for example. These 'sight' blinds will teach pup to take a straight line and starts to instill the trust in you that you really do know where the birds are. Only when you gain pup's trust will you start working as a team.

Don't do any *cold* blinds (pup doesn't see where you put the bumpers) until pup is solid on his baseball drills.

Clockwork

The clock drill (diagram 18-1) teaches pup is to both take a line and to learn to ignore the distractions of other bumpers. You and pup are in the middle of the clock and you toss six bumpers about 20 yards out, all the way around you. Think of a clock and throw one at twelve o'clock, one at two, one at four o'clock, etc. Imaginary hands of the clock are the *lines* pup will take to each bumper. Face one of the bumpers, tell pup, "Dead bird" and when he is lined up, send him. When pup comes back, heel him in the same direction and toss the bumper back out where it was. Say, "No bird" and wheel pup around to the next bumper in your clock. If he takes off for the last bumper thrown, *no* him off of it and re-heel him. Don't let him get any bumper except the one you send him for.

As pup gets proficient at the clock, lengthen the distances and then change to orange bumpers. Mix up your drills (baseball, lining and clockwork) to keep pup on his toes and to keep him from getting bored.

Treading Water

Most dogs come by this ability naturally, others have a hard time figuring out how to stay in one place. Usually, with time, the dog will figure out how to tread water. If not, you may have success by getting in the water with pup and supporting his belly while holding him in a stationary position. Pup needs to be used to you in the water with him or he may freak out and scratch the heck out of you. If you are going to try to show pup how to tread water, spend a little time with him in the water to get him used to the idea.

Water Lining Drill

The best way to work the lining drill in water is if you have access to a small pond or a corner of a larger pond where you can place bumpers about 30 yards apart on the bank. To get pup swimming across, first show pup where the bumpers are. Start off with one pile of bumpers to get pup used to taking a line in water. As you add new stations, walk around and drop two or three bumpers at the new station and toss one bumper up in the air so that it lands on the bank. Leave a few bumpers in the first station. No him off the number one station and line him for the second. When you first start this drill, put out bumpers in what will be the third station so that there is a wide gap between the two. So, pup has bumpers on the bank about 60 yards apart. Work back and forth between the two piles.

Next lesson, start pup out with the bumpers already in place at stations one and three. Refresh his memory by having him get one bumper from each area. If he gets confused, walk around and show him which bumper you want him to retrieve. Walk back around and send him. Once pup is solid on two stations, add a third in between the first two. Make sure you have at least 30 yards between each station. If pup launches toward the middle bumper and then changes his mind and goes after the left-hand bumper, heel him back and re-send him. Do NOT cast him to the other bumpers yet. You want him to take and maintain a straight line to and from the bumpers. As pup gets proficient at this drill, add at least two more stations and work pup on taking a line to each one.

Lastly, you will alternate between orange and white bumpers and then all orange bumpers.

T's and Double T's

T's and Double T's are casting drills (see diagram 18-2.) The ideal ground for this drill is a field or yard where the grass has grown about a foot tall and you can mow paths in the grass. If you can do this, mow a straight line up to 100 yards. Cross the 'T' in the middle to form a lower case "t" and mow about 30 yards to each side. Then cross it again three-quarters of the way to the end. (See diagram) What you will have is a path to keep pup on the straight and narrow that will aid him in taking crisp casts.

You can do this without all the mowing, but mowing straight lines makes it easier to keep pup on line when you introduce this drill.

Put all twelve white bumpers at the end of the straight stretch (or at about 100 yards if you aren't using the mowed method). Starting at about halfway, send pup for six of them, moving back with each retrieve. Now, sit pup and leave him to plant the six bumpers. Let pup watch you as you toss three bumpers to the ends of the first 't' or at about 30 yards from the starting point.

Send pup to the end like in a lining drill. When he returns, line him up for the long bumpers, send him and toot the whistle for a sit when pup reaches the arm of the 't'. Send pup in either direction with an *over*. The next cast, send pup all the way to the end pile of bumpers. You don't want pup to start *popping* (stopping and looking at you for directions before you blow the whistle) so you will send pup straight to the end more often that you will cast him to either side. Mix up the times you toot the whistle so pup doesn't anticipate – one long, one short, two long, two short to either side, three long, two short to one side – you get the idea.

Don't let pup get sloppy on his sits. If he casts to the wrong direction, sit him and re-cast him. If he gets out of the 'path' toot him in to you until he can make a crisp, straight line to the bumpers.

Once pup is taking every cast on the single 't', add bumpers to the upper arm of the "T." If you aren't using a mowed area, this may get confusing to pup. Make sure the bumpers are at least 30 yards from base of the 'T' and 40 yards distance from the shorter arm of the first 't'.

Sometimes you will stop pup at the first arm, sometimes you will send him all the way to the end, sometimes you will cast him over on the second arm of the 'T'. *Always* end with sending pup all the way to the end without stopping him.

Water Baseball

Water baseball is played almost like on land with the exception that you can't walk pup out to the pitchers' mound so pup has to be taking casts before starting this drill. Find a small pond, preferably one about 50 yards wide and about 80 yards long. If you don't have a small pond you will only be able to do this drill on calm days so the wind doesn't blow the bumpers out of position. Sit pup in the middle of the short side of the pond. You walk around and let pup watch you plant six white bumpers directly across from pup. Walk back around and send pup for a few of the bumpers. With pup sitting at 'home base' let him watch you walk around and plant three bumpers on the shore of the middle of each side bank and replace the few bumpers pup has already picked up from across the pond. Send pup for the straight across pile first. Next cast, send pup straight across but this time toot for pup to stop and look at you. Cast him over to either side. Have an extra bumper handy in case you have to toss one in the direction you want pup to go.

Don't be too concerned right now if pup isn't treading water well. He will get the idea with practice.

If pup tries to return by land, stop the lessons and go back to simple angle entries and returns. If you don't care about pup running the bank, then continue the handling lessons.

Work the water baseball the same as the 'T' drill on land. Mix up the casts and send him all the across more often than not. Once in a while throw in a *back* cast so pup doesn't forget how to go back. The first few lessons, give pup leeway if he seems confused. Be prepared with an extra bumper you can throw in the direction pup was cast if he gets 'lost'.

116

Tips:

When handling pup check to see what is behind you. If you are wearing camo and have trees behind you the pup may not be able to see your arm signals. This isn't a factor with yard work as much as it is in the field or at hunt tests. To help pup see your casts clearly, push your sleeves up to show your arms.

At hunt tests when there are judges and the gallery to contend with, make sure your dog is looking at you before casting.

Don't cast on the 'fly'. Give pup a chance to turn, sit, and look at you before casting. When in the water, let pup come to a standstill and tread water before casting.

Just Ducky's Justacrooner - "Bing"

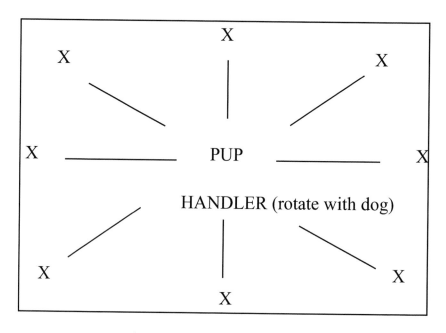

Diagram 18-1: Clock Drill

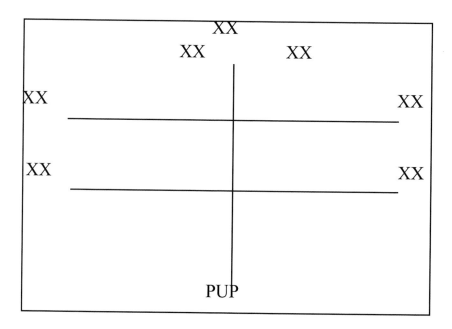

Diagram 18-2: Double T Drill

Chapter 19

Advanced Blind Retrieves

The following drills are added for those who are looking for more precise handling work from their dogs. This precision is needed if you plan on running pup in hunt test, particularly the higher levels. Pup will be expected to swim 100 plus yards, past points on of land, through flooded timber, run up and down hills, and through cover changes to get the bird. There will be plenty of distractions to pull pup off his line, so the more drills and the more complicated you make them (and get pup to listen) the better you both will do at hunt tests. Just remember to build on each new drill gradually and make sure pup understands what you expect from him.

Thread the Needle

This drill teaches pup to go through distractions. Start off with two white bumpers placed about 30 yards apart. Sit pup down in between the two bumpers and toss several white bumpers out in front of you. Heel pup back about 10 yards and set him up for the blind by telling him, "Dead bird" and "Good" when he's lined up. He should go straight to the pile of bumpers. If he wants to go to the bumpers off to the sides, *no* him and heel him back. Move closer to the pile if you need to. You will gradually move back until pup is running through the side bumpers to the pile without hesitating. When pup gets good at this drill, move the side bumpers closer together until they are about 10 yards apart and change the pile of bumpers to orange ones.

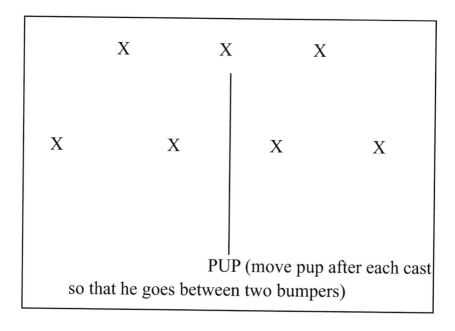

Diagram 19-1: Thread the Needle Drill

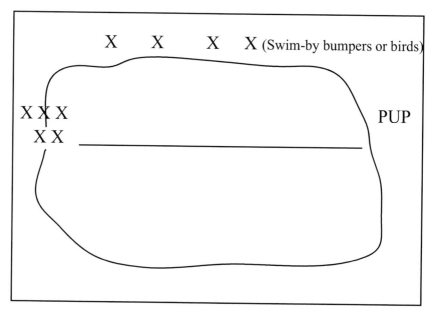

Diagram 19-2: Swim-By Water Drill

This drill can be made tougher with more bumpers. Use four white bumpers lined up about 10 yards apart. Place three orange bumpers about 20 yards out and spaced so that they are in between the white bumpers, like a pyramid (See diagram 19-1). You are going to line pup up in the open space between two of the white bumpers so that you are in line with one of the orange ones, and send pup through the 'hole' to fetch. As pup gets better at this drill, move back and move the orange bumpers further away.

Lining Drills and Swim-by's in Water

Using the same principle as Threading the Needle on land, you want pup to swim past any distractions and maintain a straight line in water.

Use the shoreline of a pond, preferably a fairly straight side of the pond, where pup can swim up to 100 yards. Sit pup and leave him watching you. Place a pile of white bumpers about 30 yards away from the edge of the bank pup is going to swim past, on land. Walk back to pup, line him up and send him. Do not let him go to the bank and run around. If the land is too tempting, move pup and the bumpers further down the pond. To make land less tempting at first, shorten the distance by putting the fetch pile of bumpers in water. This is only possible on a calm day as wind will blow the bumpers out of position.

When pup is going straight to the bumpers and back, move closer to the side bank until pup will swim the length of the pond to and from the pile of bumpers without touching land. Keep moving closer until he reaches the pile and he maintains the line only 10 yards from the bank.

Next you will place white bumpers on the long side of the shoreline (see diagram 19-2). Move pup back to 30 yards from the shore and send him across. He will see the white bumpers and be tempted to turn to pick one up. Don't let him! Keep working pup at this drill until you can move to within 10 yards of the distraction bumpers and pup maintains his line.

Get really tough and put birds in the swim-by positions. Keep pup excited by using birds in his retrieve pile as well.

Angle Backs

Amaze your hunting buddies by teaching pup how to take an angle back both in water and on land. Pup knows straight back and over, now you are going to teach him to take a 45-degree angle back.

Go back to your baseball area (use the place platform if you like) and sit pup facing you. Back up and toss a bumper over pup's shoulder at a 45-degree angle.

When you cast pup, your arm is going to be raised at the same 45 degrees. Pup will eventually learn to distinguish between straight back, over, and angle back.

Take your time with pup. When he understands left-hand angle back, work on the right side. When he seems to grasp both, toss bumpers at both positions and work pup taking casts to either side. Keep on your toes and make sure pup spins in the direction of the cast.

To teach pup in water, start off on the shoreline, pup sitting with his back to the pond. Toss one over his shoulder and cast him, remembering to keep pup turning in the direction of the cast. When pup seems to understand, work the angle backs into your water baseball drill.

Dogs are left and right 'handed' so you have to teach pup to turn in the direction of the cast. If pup wants to always turn right, spend more time emphasizing the left turn angle back. You may have to sit pup angled toward the left in order to get him to turn that way. *No* him when he turns wrong and keep at it until he grasps the concept. Be patient! Repeat from the beginning in water by placing pup on the shoreline at first until he consistently turns in the proper direction.

Wagon Wheel

Putting all the directions together takes one more drill, the Wagon Wheel. Sit pup in the center of an area where you can throw bumpers 30 plus yards to the side and behind him. Like the clockwork drill, but this time pup is at the center and you are facing him, about 20 yards away. Have pup watch you toss the bumpers for each of the casts you will make, over to each side, straight back and angles to each side. Have an extra bumper to throw.

Sit pup, facing you and begin with the easy stuff, sending pup on his *overs*. When pup brings the bumper to you, command the drop, and walk pup back to his position in the center of the wheel. Next, send pup straight back. Just like in the clockwork drill, toss each bumper back in its place after pup delivers it to hand. When you send pup for the first angle back, he is likely to go over or back (whichever direction he last came from.) *No* him, sit him back in the center and toss a bumper in the direction you want pup to go. Make sure he spins in the correct direction.

Repetition is the Key to Success

Mix up and repeat the drills as often as needed until pup takes every cast. Take your time and allow the dog to sit before casting. Don't let pup anticipate your moves and start moving before you give the signal. After you toot for the sit, count, 'one-thousand-one, one-thousand-two' to yourself to keep from sending pup too quickly.

With all of the drills, lengthen the distances and change to orange bumpers to train pup to believe in you when you send him out for a blind retrieve. This all takes hours, days, and months of patience so don't expect it to happen overnight. Working every day with a very intelligent dog you can teach the basics in a couple of months. Putting it all together and gaining pup's trust takes much longer so don't get frustrated. It will happen and when it all comes together there is no greater feeling of accomplishment.

HR UH JK Hershey's Kiss

Chapter 20
The First Hunt

One of the first things to consider before sending pup out for the first bird of the season is, does pup know what he's hunting for? If you have been training with pigeons and go dove hunting, you may have to go out and show him what a dove is. Some pups will pick it up and refuse to bring it back. Don't panic. Pick up the bird, tease pup with it and toss it a few feet for him. That should be all it takes for him to get the idea.

The same thing goes for any new game bird. How is pup supposed to know what a chukar smells like if he's never encountered one before?

Go with a friend and let her do the gunning while you handle your pup. If you are dove hunting in a field with a lot of guns, find a spot as far away from everyone as you can get. The less confusion the better. Put yourself in pup's place. Think how you would feel going to a strange field and all of a sudden 40 guns go off, dogs are running in the field, whistles are blowing, and hunters are yelling at their dogs (who broke and are running rampant) to come "HERE, dagnabit!" It can be a bit intimidating at the least.

The best bet is to go to a small field with only a few hunters (and no other dogs nearby) and take the time to work your pup. You will have years of hunting together. Use this first season to set the right tone.

Make sure to have plenty of water for pup. Take 1 and 2 liter soda bottles, fill them almost full with water and freeze. They work great in the crate and the field. As they melt you have fresh drinking water for both of you.

In cold water hunting, get pup a neoprene vest and have it altered so that it fits snugly. This doesn't mean you can work your spaniel like a Labrador or Chesapeake bay retriever. Most spaniels have coats that soak up the water rather than repel it and are not the best choice if you do a lot of duck hunting in big water or frigid temperatures. Boykin spaniels are notorious for their heart and drive and depend on you to have the common sense to know when to quit. This goes for extreme heat as well as cold weather hunting.

Be sure that pup is steady and on a check cord so that he doesn't get out in front of the guns and get shot or get deafened from the blast. The short check cord works great since you can stand on the end to remind pup to stay and still have your hands free. It won't stop a pup that isn't steady, you will have to hold him with both hands and brace yourself if he breaks. If pup isn't steady, let your buddy do the gunning while you handle pup.

Allow pup two or three hunts to get the idea of the game and an entire season to figure out what you want. He needs to see the birds fall in order to mark and retrieve them. A lot of dove shoots are along tree lines or in fields with paths cut through the corn and sunflowers. This can make it difficult for the pup to mark the falls. You may find yourself walking out with pup, encouraging him to *hunt dead*. Don't be discouraged if you find the bird before pup does. If that happens, don't pick it up. Consider the scenting conditions. If it's dry and there isn't a breeze, pup will have a hard time finding the dove. Keep talking to pup, encourage him to *find the bird*. When he does, praise pup as if he'd found a million dollars.

Of course if you are in a boat and duck hunting it would be difficult to walk out with pup. You would have to have introduced pup to a duck beforehand. If pup does not see the bird fall and the cover is heavy with reeds or lily pads, don't send him unless you have some shotgun shells or rocks to throw for pup to get him to swim out in the area. Otherwise you will just have a dog swimming around aimlessly, possibly getting tangled in and worse case, retrieving a decoy. If pup is handling blind retrieves it's another story. We are talking about a novice pup here.

The main thing to keep in mind during pup's first hunting season is to use each outing like a continuing education class. Whenever possible, have another hunter with you so that you can concentrate on showing pup what to do and how to do it. This will be time well spent for a great future of teamwork and hunting success.

ESS Timberdoodle's Freckles
photo by Lori DeMott

SHR Just Ducky's Justdoit - "Nike"
Rock'n Creek Bird Boy x HR Just Ducky's Justasample

Chapter 21

Final thoughts

Hunt Tests

There are retriever games you can play with your spaniel to keep him sharp. If you work year around training your pup you both will have fun and enjoy the hunting seasons that much more as you work as a team.

Register your pup with the **United Kennel Club** and go to some Hunting Retriever tests. The Started class is for novice handlers and/or dogs. The pup can be held on lead and doesn't have to be steady. The delivery is to a designated area and the pup doesn't have to deliver to hand. Pup does have to pick up ducks and/or pigeons, be introduced to the gun and been worked past decoys. If pup passes four Started tests he earns his SHR (Started Hunting Retriever) title.

The Seasoned class is for the more polished retriever. Pup has to be steady and deliver to hand. You, the handler, shoot the shotgun, firing blanks at the birds thrown by birdboys. There are double marked retrieves on land and water. Pup also must be competent in blind retrieves, though the distances are only about 40 yards both on land and in the water. A few other tests included are the walk-up and the diversion. When pup has accumulated forty points he earns his HR (Hunting Retriever) title.

The Finished class is tough, especially for spaniels. The triple marked retrieves can consist of three marks up to 150 yards each. The blind retrieves can be 125 yards on land and 100 yards on water. There is an honor as well as the walk-up and diversion marks. It can and is done all the time, mostly by Labrador, Chesapeake bay and Golden retrievers, with Labs dominating. The smaller spaniels are at a definite disadvantage since sometimes they can't even see the marks. Also, if the cover is high, you can't see your dog to handle her. Getting a spaniel to take a line for 50 yards is tough; try getting one to go a hundred yards! I am not trying to discourage anyone. Go for it. If Curlee Gurlee can do it, so can your pup. See the appendix for a list of Boykin and other spaniels who have earned their HR and HRCH titles thus far and get some inspiration. Just realize that it takes hours, days, months and years of training. You and your spaniel have to work like a team. She has to trust you when you say the bird really is to the left when she wants to go to the bush on the right.

The North American Hunting Retriever Club (NAHRA) is also an option in some areas. Dogs competing earn Working Retriever (WR) and Master Hunting Retriever (MHR) titles.

Both UKC and NAHRA have Grand levels of competition. I would love to see a spaniel achieve one of these extremely difficult titles.

AKC also offers retriever hunt tests though only the Irish water spaniel is accepted to run them since the Irish is classified as a retriever.

If you live near South Carolina and own a Boykin spaniel, you may consider joining the **Carolina Boykin Spaniel Retriever Club**. The CBSRC holds six hunt tests each year. The dogs earn placement ribbons and points toward Dog of the Year awards in each division - Puppy, Novice, Intermediate and Gun Dog. The classes are comparable to UKC's Started, Seasoned and Finished levels of testing.

E-collar

The electronic collar is another tool in dog training. There are no secrets to its use, just rules of behavior. If you are the type of person who loses his temper easily and takes out your anger on your dog or other people, do **not** use an e-collar. You will end up ruining a perfectly good dog and probably blame it all on the dog.

If, on the other hand, you are a compassionate, thinking individual, whose only concern is the welfare of your dog, then the e-collar can be a *tool* to be used in your training program. Before using an e-collar read all the books, watch available videos, and use the collar on yourself to see what your dog is feeling. That's right, hold the collar firmly in your hand with the prongs in your palm. Push the button activated on level one. Go as far as you like to feel the different stimulation. If you can't bring yourself to 'nick' your hand, why would you subject your dog to it?

E-collars can be utilized in the field with a hard-driving dog to keep her honest. Most of the time the dog only needs a reminder to keep her in line. For the well-trained dog that is properly collar conditioned, the occasional 'nick' is all that is needed. Most spaniels can be kept in control with your tone of voice and a check cord.

I never used an e-collar on any dog until Curlee displayed a behavior I couldn't control. She would take a beautiful, straight line to a blind. She would run over a 100 yards, actually maintaining the line and keep on going. I couldn't get her to stop! This was a good problem but one I couldn't solve by running out in the field (I couldn't run fast or far enough) to enforce the sit. Unfortunately, I didn't introduce the collar to Curlee correctly and so now, she is 'collar-wise'. If you decide to use an electronic collar, read the materials and take the time to condition your dog to the collar. If you don't then she will behave when the collar is on her and won't when the collar is off. That's fine for a hunting dog, but a trial dog that learns she can get away with misbehaving at a hunt test will definitely learn how to push *your* buttons.

Without an electronic collar you may have to exert yourself more in order to get the corrections needed. That means running out in the field and wading in the pond to get to your dog. Even if you decide to use an e-collar you will still need to touch base with your spaniel.

The collar is not a cure-all for dog training. Of course, if you have kept track of your pup's progress and always set her up for success then minimal corrections of any kind will be needed.

Nike with author at hunt test in Florida - Carl Nock and Bob Cox judging
Nike earned a pass toward her HR title
photo by Pat Trichter-Deeley

Glossary

Anti-banking - Training session to teach pup not to run along the bank either on the fetch or the return to the handler.

Bird Boy - A person who throws birds or bumpers at a hunt test - usually boys but girls and adults are welcome to play as well.

Blind - 1) a retrieve when the dog does not know where the bird is and the handler does. The dog is handled to the bird using whistle commands and hand signals. 2) Portable camouflage blind used as holding area used at hunt tests and to hide the bird boys and wingers.

Break - The dog leaves your side before being sent. A Controlled Break is when you can call the dog back to heel. An Uncontrolled Break is when the dog ignores your whistle or yell to "SIT" and goes after the bird.

Bumper/Dummy - rubber or canvas throwing device used to train retrievers.
Dokken Dead Fowl - are the latest dummies that are shaped like ducks, dove, quail, and pheasant with bird scent injected. *Dokken* have soft bodies that are easy for dogs to handle and heads on rope so that the dog is discouraged from shaking the bird (the head smacks the dog on the face.)

Check Cord - Rope used to keep pup in check. Rope should be free of knots so it doesn't tangle in brush. Several check cords in varying lengths can be used depending on pup. A long, 25 foot rope for starting pup and short lines to remind pup to remain steady.

Clicker - Small plastic box with metal tab that 'clicks'. Some will remember it as a "Cricket" toy. Used as a marker to tell the dog he did a behavior right. Also tells handler whether his or her timing needs work.

Diversion - Hunt Test term - same as Modified Double. Dog is returning with a bird when another bird is shot in the field. Dog should deliver first bird before going after the next one. A failure to do so is called a 'Switch'.

Dokken Dead Fowl - see bumper

Double - Two birds down in the field for pup to retrieve. Not shot at the same time at hunt tests but definitely possible in a hunting situation.

Finished - Third level in UKC hunt test categories. Dogs in the finished level are expected to retrieve triple marks on land and water, handle on blinds up to 125 yards, be steady on diversions and walk-ups and honor another dog working .

GRHRCH - Grand Hunting Retriever Champion - the highest level awarded by UKC/HRC. Requires 300 HRC points of which 80 must be earned by passing two Grand Hunt Tests.

Holding Blind - Camouflage material held together with two or three poles. Used at hunt tests to hide the wingers and bird boys as well as a place to wait your turn to run your dog.

HR - Hunting Retriever title earned at hunt tests sanctioned by the UKC/HRC. Requires forty (40) points.

HRC, Inc - Hunting Retriever Club - A division of the United Kennel Club, developed by hunters for hunters as a way to have fun working your dogs and to evaluate their abilities.

HRCH - Hunting Retriever Champion title. Requires one hundred (100) points.

Honor - To remain steady while another dog works.

Jackpot - Clicker training term. A bunch of treats given at one time as an extra bonus for responding to command correctly.

Line - 1) An imaginary straight line that you want your dog to maintain on his way to a blind or marked retrieve.
2) The starting point at hunt test. Often the judges will mark the area with branches or spray paint on the ground. The working dog must start behind the line.

Line Manners - The way the dog behaves on the way to the line at a hunt test. Is he heeling quietly or running out in front out of control?

Marked Retrieve - A bird/bumper that the dog sees fall.

Modified Double - Pup is returning with a bird when another bird is shot in the field. Also called a diversion in hunt tests.

Seasoned - Level of competition at HRC hunt tests. Dogs in the Seasoned level are required to do double retrieves on land and water, blind retrieves, walk-ups and diversions. Each Seasoned pass earns ten (10) points toward the HR title. Once the dog has earned the HR he or she can continue to compete but the points don't count. Forty points are required for an HR title - 10 of which can come from the Started class.

SHR - Started Hunting Retriever - UKC/HRC title earned by dogs who complete four Started tests.

Started - First level of competition at HRC hunt tests. Dogs are required to retrieve two birds on land and two birds on water, all single retrieves. Dog is not required to be steady and can be held. Dogs are not required to deliver to hand, only to an area designated by the judges. Each pass earns five (5) points. A total of ten (10) points can be earned toward the HR title. Four passes earns an SHR title.

Steady - To remain at heel, or in a designated place, until sent to retrieve, no matter if a bird has fallen, guns are being fired, or anther dog is sent for the retrieve.

Switch - Pup gives up on hunt, changes fields, and goes after second (or third) bird down before picking up first bird while working a double or triple.

Triple - Three birds down at one time. Rare in *my* duck blind but a regular occurrence at hunt tests.

U.K.C. - United Kennel Club

Walk-up - Part of hunt test scenario where dog is at heel as you walk up on hunt, bird boy throws a bird out in front of you, you shoot and pup has to remain steady until sent.

Winger - a device used to launch birds or bumpers in the air. Some are manually operated and others can be set off by remote control.

Dax and the author walking
off-line after a successful hunt test
series

photo by Pat Trichter-Deeley

Recommended Reading and Surfing

Deeley , Martin. *Working Gundogs:: An Introduction to Training and Handling,* England, Crowood Press 1994

Dobbs, Jim and Phyllis. *Tri-Tronics Retriever Training* Tucson Arizona, Tri-Tronics, Inc. 1993

Donaldson, Jean. *Culture Clash* Berkley, CA, James & Kenneth, 1996

Milner, Robert. *Retriever Training for the Duck Hunter* Long Beach, CA, Safari Press,1985

Pryor, Karen. *Don't Shoot the Dog* New York, NY, Bantam Books,1999

Walters, D.L. and Ann. *Training Retrievers to Handle* LaCygne, Kansas, D.L. Walters, 1979

Web Sites:

www.boykinspaniel.org - **The Boykin Spaniel Society**

www.boykinspaniel.com - **Pam's Boykin Spaniel Web Site**

www.boykinspaniel.com/CBSRC.html - **Carolina Boykin Spaniel Retriever Club**

www.ukcdogs.com - **United Kennel Club**

www.nahra.org/ - **North American Hunting Retriever Association**

www.offa.org - **OFA - Orthopedic Foundation for Animals**

www.vmdb.org - **CERF - Canine Eye Research Foundation**

www.vet.upenn.edu/pennhip - **PennHIP**

www.starfire-rapport.com - **Steve Rafe - Gun-Shy tapes**

www.duckdecoys.com - **Blackwater Decoys**

Spaniels with Hunt Test Titles

Boykin Spaniels

HRCH UH King's Curlee Gurlee - owned/handled by Pam Kadlec

HRCH MHR Pocotaligo's Coffee - owned/handled by Kim Parkman

HRCH UH Pocotaligo's Bailey - owned by Jule and Kim Parkman

HRCH Patton's Holy Moses - owned by JoWayne Patton

HRCH Irene's Fancy Girl - owned by Burke H. Dial

HRCH Clark's Sam - owned by Robin Clark

MHR Bette's LuLu - owned by Ivey Summrell

HR Just Ducky's Justasample - owned/handled by Pam Kadlec

HR Just Ducky's Tourbillion - owned/handled by Chris Meurett

HR Barthalomew - owned/handled by Gina Vecchione

HR Fancy's Mighty Sampson - owned/handled by Gene Putnam

HR Philly of Pocotaligo - owned/handled by Kim Parkman

HR UH Sydney of Woodbine - owned by Jake Rasor, Jr.

HR Pistol Pete Fetchum - owned/handled by Robert H. Cox

HR Hi-Brass Harley - owned/handled by Kevin K. Freeman

HR P.K. Maxwell Smart - owned/handled by Patty Labbe

HR Joe's Alabama Bear - owned by Joe Cox

SHR Just Ducky's Justdoit - needs one pass for HR owned/handled by Pam Kadlec

American Water Spaniels

HR UH JK Hershey's Kiss - owned/handled by Jeff Kraynik

SHR UH Waterway's Dax WD - owned by Haydee & Allan Kozich

HR UH SR CH Game Creek's Barrel O'Bourbon WDX, CGC owned/handled by Kevin Smith

Sussex spaniel

CH. Sundowners Swing That Music, JH (aka Satch) - owned by Jan Euphrat Hepper

Irish Water Spaniels

UCDX Saracen's Bold to the Bone CDX JH WCX CGC

Ch. Yeates of Lisnabrogue CD TD MH WCX (first IWS to earn the AKC MH title) - Owned by Elissa Kirkegard

WR Ch. Jaybren's Aran UD SH WCX - Owned by Jim Brennan

Ch. Jaybren's Siobhan UD TD SH WCX - Owned by Jim Brennan

WR Ch. Whistlestop's Irish Ace CD SH WCX - Owned by Katie Seitz DVM

Ch. Jaybren's Bonnie Rioghnach CD SH WCX - Owned by Jim Brennan

Ch. Jaybren's Donnchadh Dona CDX SH NAJ MX WCX
Owned by Jim Brennan

Ch. Madcap's Rising Star Stella CDX MH WCX CGC (first IWS bitch to earn the AKC MH title) - Owned by Rosemary Sexton

Ch. Jaybrens Hi-Five Dhochas Mor CDX TD SH OAJ OA WCX
Owned by Christine Robertson MD

Wh'Stop-Saracen's Highlander MH WCX - Owned by Greg and Marcia Thudium and Susan Sarracino-Diehl

Ch. Muddy Waters Carey O'Birdhill CDX SH TD WC - Owned by Mary Reich

O'Malleigh's High Jinks Deegan SH WCX CGC - Owned by Misalyn Armstrong

Ballyhoo's Crystal Whistle SH - Owned by Jack and Colleen McDaniel

SHR Saracen's Tule Bog CD SH TDI - Owned by Mary Ruth Calhoun

Ballyhoo's Brown Ale, SH - Owned by Karen & Joe Quinn

MHR Beachbouy Dailin JH CD WCX - Owned by Hyla Mendelow
Dailin is the only IWS to earn the NAHRA MHR title. He also has 3 legs on the AKC MH and the CKC MH titles.

Just Ducky Kennel Brags Page

HRCH UH King's Curlee Gurlee

1997, 1999, 2002 Boykin Spaniel Society's National Open Champion
Whelped 4/22/94 - Conformation: Good - Size: Fair (28lbs of pure
energy, 14 1/2 inches at shoulder) - Temperament: Excellent
    1995 2nd place Puppy BBS National Hunt Test
    1995 2nd place Novice BBS National Hunt Test
    1995 3nd place Intermediate BBS National Hunt Test
1996 Earned her UKC Hunting Retriever title before age of 2
    1996 JAM Open BBS National Hunt Test
    1997 BSS National Open Champion
March, 1998 - HRCH title at Midlands HRC Hunt Test
    1998 4th place Open BSS National Hunt Test
    1999 BSS National Open Champion
    2000-2001 CBSRC Gun Dog of the Year
    2002 - UH title earned in 4 consecutive upland tests
    2002 - BSS National Open Champion

HR Just Ducky's Justasample

HRCH UH King's Curlee Gurlee x HR UH Sydney of Woodbine
Whelped 6/3/97 - 35lbs. 17" at shoulder - OFA Good - BY-535G28F-T
    1998 BSS National Champion Puppy
    1998-1999 CBSRC Novice Dog of the Year
    1999-2000 CBSRC Intermediate Dog of the Year
Dam of HR Just Ducky's Tourbillion and SHR Just Ducky's Justdoit

Just Ducky's Sir Jaymes Mark

Rock'n Creek Bird Boy x HRCH UH King's Curlee Gurlee
1999 BSS National Champion Puppy

Strick's Just Ducky Tao

HRCH UH King's Curlee Gurlee x HR UH Sydney of Woodbine
2000 BSS National Champion Novice

Index

Note: Numbers in bold refer to photographs

JUST DUCKY

P U B L I S H I N G

P.O. Box 129
720 Plum Branch Road
Edgefield, SC 29824
803- 637-2007
FAX - 803-637-5825
pam@boykinspaniel.com

<u>*Retriever Training for Spaniels*</u>
by Pamela Owen Kadlec

Ordering Information

Name: _____

Address: _____

City, State, Zip Code: _____

Phone: _____

If requesting an autographed copy - name of recipient(s):

_____

Please send _____ copies @ $19.95 + $5.00 shipping for one book
- add 2.00 per book for additional shipping
SC Residents please add 6% sales tax _____

Total: _____

Please e-mail or call for discount information when ordering three or
more books.

Thank you!
Pamela O. Kadlec